# Recovery/Discovery

# Jason Tune &
# Tina Morgan

**chipmunkapublishing**
the mental health publisher

Published by
Chipmunkapublishing
United Kingdom

**http://www.chipmunkapublishing.com**

Copyright © 2014 Jason Tune & Tina Morgan

ISBN    978-1-78382-134-1

Chipmunkapublishing gratefully acknowledge the support of Arts Council England.

**Acknowledgements**

I would like to publically thank the following for their help with this book and in my life. In no particular order or preference, I am eternally grateful to Tina Morgan who has co-written this book with me, despite her busy schedule and motherhood. She gave her time and commitment to this adventure.

I also want to thank her husband James Morgan for helping me to proof read this book and I appreciate his constructive criticisms as positive and not personal, to enable the book to grow.

A special thanks to Kevin Williamson, Nutritionist, Simon Cant, Secretary and David McMullan, Deputy Manager / Social Worker Practitioner and my other colleagues at the Early Intervention Team in Rotherham for supporting this project. I am forever grateful for the opportunity to become a health care professional with the Rotherham, Doncaster and South Humber Mental Health NHS Foundation Trust and service users connected to the trust who I have met down the years.

I would like to personally thank Karen Etheridge, Malcolm Peet, Justin Morley, John Coates, Paul McCrea, Syed Hussain, Dave Scarrott, Nick Arkell, Phil Proudman, Chris Bain, Cheryl Watkinson, Monica Deakin friends and colleagues who believed in me.

People at Rotherham United Football Club, my own town football club.

Chris Cooper, my special friend who has supported me throughout my publications.

Rotherham Advertiser (Rotherham local newspaper), Radio Sheffield.

Steve Smith (Solicitor) for his advice when I first thought about writing about my experiences.

I also appreciate my friends throughout life who have put up with me through the trying and difficult times and gave me their support and have stood the test of time. I am glad I have met new friends who continuously appreciate me for being me and my endeavours to help people overcome their difficulties. I want to thank my friends at 'Shirecliffe Spiritual Circle of Friends' in Sheffield that my partner Sharon and I facilitate and other friends in the spiritual circles that I have met in the last few years.

I want to give special thanks to my family for their unconditional love that without I wouldn't be who I am today. Also, remembering those have passed in my family and friends who I will never forget.

I want to thank my inspirational friend and publisher, Jason Pegler C/O of Chipmunkapublishing and his team in London, for believing in me and giving me an opportunity to share my journey with the wider audience.

I would also like to mention my pal from the same area as me, Kev McCourt, a recently retired school teacher, who initially invited me to his school to do a talk about my mental health experiences. Kev is now passionate about de stigmatizing mental ill health. Kev raises awareness, and he networks from an education perspective about mental health.

I also appreciate Nicky Jones creative artist and friend, who made a rap on my behalf, see YouTube Chipmunkapublishing (Stigma worse than Psychosis)

I am also very grateful for my GP's and nurses at my doctor's surgery and also the surgeons who have helped me at Rotherham District General Hospital regarding several operations I have had as a patient.

The consultants and mental health workers who have helped me during my time as a service user.

Ray Gray a.k.a Sam, Simon Currie, Dave & Paul Douglas, Mick and Tommy Wilson, Roy Adrell, Carl Swan, Ziggy. Dave Codewell, for his support at the Body Tec gym. Mick Maglan, Martin Appleyard, Neil F, Dave Gaynor, Terry (the electrician)

A special thanks to Celia my neighbour who I am eternally grateful too xx

My extended family and relations.

John & Ben Codewell.

Janet my mums bopping partner xx

Margaret Andrews and her family, the kettle is always on for a chin wag and a catch up xx

My partner's family xx

The great people and dancers I have met on the Northern Soul Scene

Kimberworth Comprehensive School for all the memories

People from my grass roots on Meadowbank estate in Rotherham Yorkshire

John Curtis, special friend.

Ryan, Wes and Steve Rhodes.

People from the Body Tec and Oasis gym's in Rotherham.

The lads from the demolition and my steel erecting days.

Also the Alpine soft drinks pals.

My son's grandparents, Ron & Angela.

The 'Rock n Roll' gang at the grange

Julie Moxon close friend

Kev Farnell my buddy

Rob & Jo Nettleton valued friends

Jean Staves close friend

Facebook friends

Last but not least, my soul mate Sharon Fenton for giving her computer up for me to write this book. She is always there for me and encourages me to continue my belief that we can all be better people by understanding others and ourselves more.

If I have not publically mentioned anyone else who has supported me, I apologise as the list could go on and never end, however I am not neglecting my feelings as I write this.

**Forward**

I am Dr Syed Hussain, a member of the Royal College of Psychiatrists in the UK, with thirteen years of experience in psychiatry. During these years I have treated individuals of various ages affected by all types of mental disorders. I met Jason Tune during my training in Rotherham, UK, in the Early Intervention in Psychosis Team, who works there as an experienced Support Time and Recovery worker in the community mental health team. While in training, I discovered that Jason had suffered from mental health issues himself, but managed to successfully overcome them. This led to our discussions about the significance and the role of spirituality, lifestyle and personal responsibility in recovery from psychosis.

'Recovery /Discovery' is a book that will benefit people with mental health issues and their carers, as it is written by a person who has faced similar problems in the past and has successfully dealt with them. Jason described his life before and after psychiatric diagnosis in his books *'Sex, Drugs and Northern Soul'* and *'Stigma Worse than Psychosis'* while the current book outlines his journey to recovery and fulfilling life. In this book Jason describes in detail how he healed himself by discovering the road to recovery through understanding his illness, preventing relapses, making important life style changes, getting employment and using spirituality as his strength.

As a doctor I come across people in similar situations and with similar life experiences as Jason's on a regular basis. As a medical professional, I endeavor to help them from medical point of view. However, Jason gives an extremely valuable input from experiential point of view, while showing great empathy towards and understanding of the patients' illness and how it affects quality of life and relationships with others. Most importantly, this book gives hope to those suffering from similar mental health problems, highlighting the fact that recovery is possible and that it is often a matter of choice rather than destiny. Jason, as an important member of the mental health team in the Early Intervention in Psychosis provides blue print of recovery to others.

I was delighted when Jason asked me to write a foreword for *'Recovery/ Discovery'* as I am a firm believer in natural ways of healing and preventing mental health illnesses through lifestyle changes such as drinking enough water, doing regular exercise, eating a healthy diet and practicing spirituality. Jason's book about his very personal experience of successfully dealing with psychosis makes him a role model and can positively contribute towards mental wellbeing of others.

Dr Syed Hussain. (MRCPsych)

**Brief Introduction**

My autobiography 'Sex, Drugs and Northern Soul' was about the journey of my life from my childhood up until approximately 40 years of age. My Sequel 'Stigma Worse than Psychosis' highlighted the stigma of having a label that I endured throughout my mental ill health history.

This book is about mental health recovery and having a positive response to some of these issues. I believe that we are all in some kind of recovery albeit from a debt, a divorce, bereavement etc... and some people may even say from life itself. I am not going to compare my experiences of recovery with anyone else's recovery, nor is what I am going to illustrate applicable to everybody. My main objective is that I will inspire hope to others that may or may not be similarly afflicted with mental health issues and belief for their carers and loved ones. This is based on personal experience throughout my life up to date.

## Chapter 1: Survival as a kid

In my childhood, I do not ever recall hearing about psychology, counselling, coping mechanisms, talking strategies or any other therapies for that matter. The word stress was never mentioned in my neighbourhood and if we had a problem we were told to "Pull ourselves together like a pair of curtains". Often it would not go with the macho language and image I was accustomed to on the rough council estate that I was raised on. I was brought up with a "Hear all see all say nothing" mentality. This was acceptable and normal to me being slightly anti-authority in my old life. I now see this attitude as detrimental to my mental health recovery that I am going to write about in the following chapters.

I would often get into trouble, naively, by protecting friends or peers at school and in other areas of my life. I had become very angry, disillusioned and hurt from being called names and verbally abused at my infant school in the late 1960s, for having a lazy eye and being on free school meals. I kept these feelings and thoughts to myself. On reflection, if I had disclosed some of the bigotry and verbal comments that were directed at me to my teachers at the infant's school, maybe my path may have taken a different turn. Sadly, that will never be known so I am not going to psycho-analyse too deep into those yester years. I will give a broad overview of my childhood as we move along with my story; I shall not be "Getting the shovel out and digging too deep".

I recall being bullied at that period of my life and saying to myself , as I looked over the infant school's wall neighbouring to the comprehensive school, that one day when I grow up I am going to be the toughest guy at the senior school and no one is ever going to pick on me again. Bearing in mind, I was wearing small shorts; I also wore national health spectacles and being five years old at the time! I don't know what the reader's imagination is like, but I can only visualise and speak for myself that I most definitely did not look like a world boxing champion. This was my first mental thought about how I was going to respond and cope with the dilemma that I was induced to at that point of my development. Here I was trying to understand my feelings from this emotional trauma.

I ended up having a fight with the biggest and allegedly the hardest kid in my peer group at the infant's school and at that time the bullying ceased in my own age band. Despite the fact that the bullying stopped in my school, I had unwittingly started other pressures and implemented a reputation on myself. For example, other kids expected me to stick up for them and fight their battles, they also used my name as a front to bully other kids and say that I was going to sort them out in a physical, aggressive way. Although I was a bright kid at school, I now realise that I was slightly side-tracked from studying things academically that I was sent to school to learn. This distracted me from focusing on my school work as well as forming genuine alliances and true friendships instead of being used.

Psychologically, it was not all bad because it gave me the status that otherwise I might not have had, for instance if I wanted to play football I could just join in any side I desired at school, without any of the kids challenging me. This made me sometimes push the boundaries more; I was not an enforcer looking for trouble but more a protector. The friends I stuck up for were sometimes less fortunate than other kids, who were also on free school meals like me and vulnerable to ridicule and bigotry.

Back then there were not many people from ethnic backgrounds in my catchment area and town. Sometimes people were just bullied because of the colour of their skin. There was a lot of prejudice regarding our vulnerabilities albeit from different perspectives, but the outcomes were similar regarding the emotional pain. In contrast, some of my peers were false friends. They could not understand our feelings and alliances amongst us, due to their different social economic circumstances at that time. We became survivors in our own sweet little way, through more a feeling of empathy rather than sympathy. We never vented our thoughts or emotions between ourselves; it was more like an intuition, an instinct, a gut feeling. I am pleased to say that some of this bonding has stood the test of time; it is like a non-verbal communication by sticking together and understanding each other's difficulties. Supporting each other rather than being on your own with the problems helped to make our early adolescent days more tolerable.

This is a reflection of my infancy and early school life and I am pleased to say I have come out of it in one piece. These survival instincts and resiliencies have helped me in my own recovery through life's ups and downs. This learnt behaviour became a pattern in my junior school days as well. I recall also being the tough guy of the junior school; I continued to stick up for some of my peers and often "Played to the orchestra" regarding my evolving reputation. I recall loving my school work at the junior school, I also enjoyed physical education, some of the projects and may I say I am not proud of it, the odd fight or two.

I was very settled living at my grandparents at that period of my life and throughout the 1970s. I sort of got the one to one as they say nowadays, meaning that I was slightly spoilt at my grandparents. What they didn't have in money, they made up with things that money couldn't buy. I had lots of love and care from them and I am eternally grateful to my grandparents for raising me to the best of their abilities, despite them both getting on in years at the time. When I reflect about my occasional hard times, I refer to people saying that not having love and other things in their childhood can affect adult life and leave them vulnerable. I want to dedicate this sentence in my grandparents memory as part of my recovery has been to reflect on what I did have and still feel in my heart from my childhood at their abode.

I guess I was getting more attention at my grandparents than I would have done at my kin folks, due to the mayhem and bedroom sharing at my parent's home. This was the first experience of me liking my own space as well, which I now value in my adult life to reflect and deliberate. The family dynamics at home included five kids, two older sisters Marina and Cheryl, then occasionally me, the middle sibling, my younger brother David, youngest sister Samantha and not forgetting my mother and father. Looking back in my life, my primary school days were probably the happiest days of my childhood.

My interest in creative writing started in my last years of primary school; I remember my summer school holidays being about six weeks at the time. I used to write about ten pages upon my return to school after the summer break. The other kids would submit an average of four pages in their notebooks, I didn't realise my ability at the time. I would transcribe about my adventures mainly in my social environment as I lived near a meadow and a canal, there were plenty of wildlife and nature in the vicinity. In those halcyon days the kids from my neighbourhood would often spend most of their school holidays down the canal bank as we used to call it and we would play on a Tarzan swing that was made out of rope. We would also climb trees, make tree houses and dens and swim in the local canal.

I am not proud to mention this, but we sometimes went bird nesting, which is stealing eggs out of the birds nest, this was a bit of a fad in my neighbourhood in those days. I really respect Mother

Nature nowadays and can I just state at this point without making any excuses, that the event of bird nesting is a childhood activity that I wished I had not participated in. There were plenty of positive adventures besides the bird nesting experience and as I say previously, I would often write about these adventures back in school. I suppose this made me stand out amongst my peers and gave me a sense of pride and wellbeing. On reflection, it was the first time I was aware of my determination to achieve.

The exam results at the end of my primary school year in 1976 had propelled me into a top set class at the comprehensive school. I recall being under some kind of peer pressure, as my older sisters Cheryl and Marina were already in the top set at the comprehensive school. I could say this was a positive peer pressure to emulate the high standards that my sisters had set. I was determined to not let the family's academic achievements down and I was allotted into the top class of my final school. However, my early days in the new school were not all about the feel good factor from getting into the 'A' form. As I mentioned previously, my childhood reputation was unfortunately going before me. I was again side-tracked and my focus on school work seemed to go on the back burner, as more and more people wanted to fight me.

At that time we had six junior schools all feeding into the comprehensive school in the catchment area. All the number one tough kids from the feeder schools wanted to fight me for the number one of the year. I initially turned some of the fights down, as I did not want to get my new school uniform dirty; I would have got ridicule at home from my parents. I was definitely not scared of these wannabes, in the end I decided that I was not going to take any more grief. My response was to stand my ground and fight; I had mixed feelings and emotions before and after these fights. If I had lost the fights these people would never been off my back. If I won, hopefully the challenges would cease. I was in a bit of dilemma and the pros outweighed the cons, so to cut a long story short, I won all my fights in my school life. On consideration, I would have been better off going to a boxing academy!

Looking back, I was starting to get adrenaline and anxiety before and after these fights. I guess there is a connection with the fight or flight theory which refers to a physiological reaction that occurs in the presence of something that is terrifying, either mentally or physically. In response to acute stress, the body's sympathetic nervous system is activated due to the sudden release of hormones. Basically, this response prepares the body to either flee or fight the threat (Cherry 2013). I was not aware of this philosophy at that time in my teens.

I have a lot more respect these days in my community and town for helping people than actually knocking them on their backsides. I feel as though I have balanced the scales back in my favour and I suppose my anger in my head has been transferred to my heart in the psychological love sense of care, compassion and understanding. One of my favourite sayings is, "The journey from the head to heart is the longest and hardest journey of all".

I am now going to digress, as anyone who knows me will tell you that I often do. Teenage life for me was regularly about rebellion and I probably was a rebel without a cause amongst many other things in those days. I had left my grandparent's house by the time my teens had started; they did not want me to stay out late. My grandparents wanted to go to bed early as they were not getting any younger, my granddad was in his late 70's and my grandma was in her mid-70's at the time. They didn't believe in latch door kids, in other words, children that were left to their own devices. They were really old-fashioned, the man goes to work and the woman stays at home and looks after the kids etc. Therefore, I had no key of my own and they were getting fed up of waiting up late for me.

I wanted to come out of my comfort zone at my grandparent's home in my teens, I stayed out late and would hang around with an older gang; we usually got up to no good. I guess reflecting back; some of my behaviour was becoming rather anti-social. I was smoking, drinking alcohol, fighting and chasing the opposite sex. My reputation had gone beyond the boundaries of my school catchment area. Some of this behaviour seemed fun throughout my adolescence. Conversely, in my naivety I now realise that I was probably masking a lot of unhappiness and other underlying emotions.

There was a lot of turmoil at my parent's home and there had also been very high expressed emotions and lots of arguments in the family dynamics. My mother and father had drifted apart and were in the middle of a divorce, I didn't comprehend their situation at that moment in my life. Sometimes I felt that I was not just the middle child but also in the centre of my parent's problems. With my wiser wisdom, I now realise I was using negative escapes to cope with the all-round situation. My reputation and false status was a survival instinct and a way of life for me in and around school. I started playing truant from school and was earning money working up to 12 hours a day doing various jobs; this went on sometimes for weeks and into months. Occasionally, I would go back to school to try and catch up on my subjects. You don't need to be a rocket scientist to guess that my grades were suffering and that I was slipping down the academic ladder in my form. Somehow I managed to stay in the top forms throughout my comprehensive school days.

My mother, who was my main guardian in my teens, was struggling to cope with her own affairs and keeping tabs on me as well. The money that I would earn while bunking off school would often be wasted on underage drinking. It was a misconception and slight delusional thinking that I was a man before I was a lad. Maybe I was doing a man's job with all the hours I was working in between school. I was also in the army cadets and I still wanted to do my cadet training to pursue a military career when leaving school. Sometimes when I returned to school, I felt that I did not fit into the school system and their curriculum.

On consideration I was very naïve and "I had my hands into too many pies" as the saying goes. I often didn't finish off things I had started, I now realise that this can cause lots of chaos in your mind, invoke stress, anxiety and other mental health problems. This would leave me anxious, depressed, stressed, confused, and sleep deprived. I didn't understand these feelings, thoughts and sentiments as I had no previous education or experience on these matters. "You can't put an old head on a young person's shoulders" my granddad used to say. I just kept on going and looking back, my sleep pattern was disoriented, I had become chaotic at times, out of control, and disempowered.

## Chapter 2: Encouraging Disclosure

In my old life as previously stated I did not disclose my thoughts and feelings to anyone. Many young kids, teenagers and adults still find it hard to open up, however, in my professional role I now encourage people I care for to talk about their issues. In the right circumstances I see this disclosure as strength and not a weakness. Some of my friends see this philosophy in me as a fundamental to my balance and continuous journey of recovery and beyond. Anyway, back to the prodromal build up to my major introduction of the world of psychiatry. Prodromal is a psychiatric terminology that describes the early stages and progression of psychosis before the manifestation of the onset of the psychotic episode and illness. So there I was in the autumn of 1980, tough guy of the school, trying to catch up with all the school work I had missed though truancy and other circumstances as previously stated.

However, what I have not mentioned is the fact that I went back to school in my last year for another reason. I guess this was due to getting deeply and emotionally attached to a childhood sweetheart. I had gone from one extreme to another from being anti-school/authority, underage drinker, gang member, staying out all night and generally being a juvenile delinquent. All of a sudden I was trying to get my act together and I had not realised how far off track I had slipped. I tried my best to get myself together without going through the fundamental processes from my chaotic behaviour, lack of insights and my mask of macho-immaturity versus my underlying undisclosed emotions, as I didn't realise that I needed professional help. I was fearless at the time and I feared nobody in my social environment and beyond. Yet here I was strutting around like a love struck Romeo and I was trying to conceal these sensations. There was a special girl that had captivated my heart, she never knew my true feelings and respect for her at the time; those feelings were not returnable from her part. The romance never really materialised and the run into Christmas 1980 was another emotional knock back that I did not know how to handle.

There had been many trigger points at that time in my life that I had no worldly wisdom or knowledge of. Historically, I have often masked my problems and negativity with alcohol and substance misuse. I think I had been anxious for most of my adolescence and had psychological issues throughout my early teens. When my lady friend at school announced that she was not interested in a relationship, I felt I did not understand the rejection and reasoning behind this learning curve. Once again I cannot reiterate the importance to talk to someone at the earliest opportunity, instead of keeping it within you, thus allowing it to suppress and manifest, otherwise as I would say it is "Living in your mind rent free", "Thank God the landlord has not been collecting for a long time". If you are not venting and not letting go, you can become tormented in your mind. "If you put enough hats one on top of another, eventually they will fall over". I did not attend school in the New Year of 1981; this was officially my school leaving year and the year that I was going to sit my G.C.S.E (General Certificate in Secondary Education) exams.

## Chapter 3: Psychiatric Admissions

A major life changing event occurred during the Christmas period of 1980, I had suffered an emotional breakdown. This was due to a build-up of masking my problems, emotions, and stress for a long period of time. It is never just one thing or one situation that triggers a breakdown or mental health problems. It certainly takes more than one coping mechanism and strategy to get on the road to recovery. The emphasis on this book is about recovery and reinventing oneself. This is how it was for me previously before my breakdown at this stage of the book.

Suddenly all the tables had been turned upside down and here I was in Rotherham Psychiatric Unit in my home town, nowadays reduced to rubble and demolished. I am pleased to say that there is a new mental health unit that is more suitable to meeting the needs of vulnerable people with acute mental health problems. I also like the idea of dropping the words psychiatric unit and using less stigmatic, institutionalised terminology at the new hospital in my town and beyond.

My experience at the time I was hospitalised was something that I still find hard to comprehend and explain. I was totally lost in this unit and I did not understand what was happening to me and why I was on the psychiatric ward. What I do know is that I refused medication as it was making me endure horrific side-effects, and the experience before I began to settle down was like something from a horror movie "Your worst nightmare come true". The staff had mostly been asylum trained and seemed to have a zero tolerance to my adolescent manic behaviour.

I regularly spent time in seclusion protesting about some of the treatment, behaviour and bad practices from some of the staff. I was often injected in my backside with an old typical medicine called, Largactil, which is now an out dated principle. It appeared to me that the staff were just as institutionalised as the patients. Largactil, also known as Chlorpromazine or Thorazine in the United States, was the first typical drug developed with specific antipsychotic action in the 1950's, mainly to treat schizophrenia, an illness that I've never been diagnosed with. I detested this antipsychotic medication because it left me feeling over sedated, inactive and gave me massive side effects of stiffness, tremors, weight gain, skin rashes, blurred vision, impotence, over salvation and it also made me constipated and nauseated. I sometimes felt like I was treading grapes as I felt I couldn't keep still, it was often known as the Largactil shuffle. I regularly refused this medication and that is why I was often locked in seclusion where the Largactil would be forcibly injected into me. I would protest against this system and I am glad to say that other similar protests have helped to reduce the use of this drug and similar drugs from a less enlightened era.

I have personally seen both sides of the equation regarding anti-psychotic medicine and am pleased to say that we have moved on as a society and the medication is a lot better with less side effects. In my professional role I have witnessed new atypical medications being prescribed, and the results have been phenomenal within a new generation with a similar disposition to me. These pharmacological interventions have been paramount in the early stages of treatment, have added, supported long and short term recovery in many people that I have rubbed shoulders with. I also see people who do not want to take prescribed treatment and occasionally non-compliant with their medication. I personally understand why people do not want to take medication. I recall being on medication myself and refusing to take the medicine whilst in the psychiatric unit. Some of the reasons that made me refuse psychiatric drugs were due to the negative side effects and the sting of the stigma that is unfortunately still sometimes associated with mental ill health.

A distant memory for me was when I put my tablets in my sock; this was because I did not want a new girlfriend to know that I was on a prescribed drug for mental illness. Back in the here and now, I see less side-effect's with the new atypical medicines now available. I encourage people to take their medication if it is prescribed by a consultant or doctor; after all, there are many people who take remedies for a range of illnesses and issues. People also use vitamins, women take birth control pills, and impotent men take Viagra. So why should people be ashamed to administer something that is going to help their recovery?

I remember the first time that I went out with a Community Psychiatric Nurse (CPN) in my present job and I was pleased to see that she was reading a leaflet to a client regarding their prescription. In my time as a service user, none of this information was given to me, to make an informed decision. I am glad to see choices given in respect of medication and often the healthcare professionals will talk about alternative treatments that are available, especially if the one prescribed is not suitable to the person. This is more to do with the person-centred approach philosophy, giving positive self-regard and as much control and empowerment to the individual.

I can reflect on some of the family work experiences that I have been involved in with my colleagues. I have seen a radical shift from everything being under clinical settings, for example, I see our doctors visiting people in their own homes with their family members present. I have gone out on home visits with consultants and doctors within the Early Intervention Team that I am employed with. It is an on-going privilege that I am proud to be involved with and have been encouraged by the clinicians to voice my opinions, views on the care planning and empowerment of service users. Down the years I have been under several psychiatrists as an inpatient and service user in the community. To be going out, supporting psychiatrists on assessments is like a "Poacher becoming gamekeeper" and makes me think that things sometimes happen for a reason. These home visits are more private and informal than going for an official appointment to a psychiatric department or hospital. The client and the family are obviously more relaxed in their own environment and also it reduces the stigma of going to a mental health department.

Being involved and working closely within the family dynamics gives you a better insight and a clearer bigger picture regarding the service user's story. The family are involved with the Care Programme Approach (CPA) which is a person-centred framework created with the service user to deliver high quality care. It aims to facilitate closer and implement integrated working, enabling a co-ordinated approach to care delivery in the recovery process. It is ideal to see someone in their own comfort zone which is less stressful and less stigmatic for the individual. A CPA is a particular way of assessing, planning and reviewing someone's mental health care needs. It is recommended that the person who needs a CPA is involved in the assessment of their own needs and in the development of the plan to meet these goals. There should be a formal written care plan which outlines any risks and details of what should happen in an emergency or crisis. A CPA care co-ordinator should be appointed to co-ordinate the assessment and planning process. In so doing, the service users are more open and interactive and more likely to engage better. The care co-ordinator is usually a community psychiatric nurse, social worker or occupational therapist.

The family can help in the recovery process of the client as they know them when they are well and when they became unwell. In addition, the family may be aware of some of the trigger points and events that have led up to the deterioration in their mental health. This information from the carer/family can help the healthcare professional to get a better picture of the patient in the assessment process. The carers/family can help empower the recovery of the service user, for example, monitoring medication, ensuring that medication is taken at the right time, right dose and report any adverse effects back to the key worker. The carer is invaluable in making sure that the medication regime is implemented and that the prescriptions are picked up at the pharmacy and appointments are attended and followed up. This is light years away from my personal experiences, as CPA's, Community Mental Health Teams (CMHT) and Early Intervention Teams (EIT) had been non-existent in my time as a service user in the early 1980s.

My family were never given the reasons why I was put on medication at the time of the onset of my first episode of psychosis. Unfortunately, I never had a full needs assessment or a care plan which could have included assessments and reviews that demonstrated individual's full needs were met, as CPA's were not in place in the early 80's . The CPA can incorporate a robust care plan, action plan, or support plan to suit the individual and is often a contract that is signed by professionals and the service user. Each has a copy of the CPA and it is reviewed regularly with the care team and may include other agencies, family members and carers. A holistic person-centred approach is essential when assessing, it is about putting a plan together to tailor the service user's needs. For example, supporting social inclusion and graded exposure which could help someone who has withdrawn and socially isolated themselves. This could be a step-by-step plan that may involve catching buses and bus training, when a person has been suffering social anxiety and acute psychosis or other mental health problems. It may also involve support around a medication plan and agreeing to engage with their workers, attending any appointments; i.e. for substances, alcohol, educational, or activity and vocational pursuits. My family never had a carers assessment whilst I was under their care; a carers assessment is a chance for a carer to discuss with their mental health team, social services department or local authority what they need help with, in regards to caring for their loved one. I was never allocated a community mental health worker in my late teens following discharge from hospital nor was my family given any support once I was back at home. However, I did get some excellent support in the community in my latter years as a service user and this input has been paramount with my family's love on my journey of recovery and beyond.

Occasionally I come across people who do not want to engage with services and are in denial and do not want treatment or support. I can empathise with their plight as I have been a service user with a similar disposition. Nevertheless I'm trying to give you the reader an insight into a predominantly recovery story, I still feel that I have a respectful duty to you, to highlight the awareness and the negative perceptions and feelings of the individual afflicted.

I have personal and professional experiences and can often empathise with people experiencing mental distress and I feel this helps me balance my role in my employment. I remember being in denial and not wanting to engage with services myself. This was due to a lack of education, the right information, less informed professionals and the stigma of having a mental illness, which I no longer endure. I am proud of coming through both the illness and the stigma. I am not ashamed of my previous mental health history as it is not my present well-being. People are proud of combating and managing physical illnesses, why shouldn't I as a mental ill-health survivor be proud of my recovery and new lease of life?

Without these experiences, I believe that I would not have the insights to understand the professional thinking and the client's point of view and where they are coming from. I feel that my empathy is invaluable in my working life, career and also in my social, personal and private life. I occasionally meet people who disclose that they have had issues outside of my working environment and "I believe that we all have mental health; however, we don't all experience severe mental illness". I consider that we are all susceptible and under duress and extreme pressure or loss we can tip the scales from balance to unbalance.

As we go along with the book, I will illustrate some of my coping mechanisms, theories, self-awareness and insights that I have gained along the journey of recovery. It is over twenty years since my last admission into hospital at the time of this book being published and I still keep a check on my mental well-being. I am still learning new coping strategies and discovering new techniques. It is a sort of prevention rather than cure philosophy. Sleep deprivation and living a chaotic lifestyle were part of the triggers and contributing factors to my ill health. It is almost second nature for me nowadays to go to bed and try and get at least six to eight hours sleep a night. I'm like most people, if I don't have enough sleep it can affect my mood and perceptions. I realise now how crazy and naïve I was for often staying awake over 3 to 4 days and nights consecutively when I was predominately a class 'A' drug user on amphetamines, I experimented with other illicit substances as well. The stress and pressure I used to put myself under, I would never dream of again in a million years!

I also eat regular meals (some people may say too regular) as I have always been a big and above average size guy (drugs aside). Sometimes when I was ill I would not eat for days, at other times when I was really low and depressed, I would eat copious amounts of unhealthy foods and I would sometimes wake up during the middle of the night and have a food binge. I am now aware of the importance of nutrition and healthy eating as part of my well-being and recovery. I do not drink caffeine and other beverages that can enhance/stimulate hyperactivity. I feel more in control and have better education of my diet. Working in the health service and being around like minded colleagues has been a good influence on me and gave me the mind set of being healthier overall.

My partner Sharon is very supportive and she also works in the NHS and is health conscious around her diet and this has helped me to lose over two and a half stones (16 kilograms) this year at the time of writing this book. I intend to lose another two and a half stone as I have put a lot of weight on in the last ten years and since I stopped cigarette smoking. I am now drug, alcohol free and nicotine clean. I feel so much better, I have a new lease on life as my outlook and aspirations are more attainable. I have more financial scope to pursue my hobbies, interests, leisure activities and also feel as though I have overcome my previous addictive habits. For instance, the money that I spent on nicotine, I now spend on a gym membership which obviously has given me a healthier lifestyle. My general wellbeing has enhanced since I have combated my addictive personality (which is open to debate?) and I don't want go into as I find too many contrasting opinions about addictive personalities.

I am not obsessive; nevertheless, I like to keep clean and tidy in my personal hygiene and in my living quarters, as the saying goes "Cleanliness is next to godliness keep in the spirit". I know what it is like to experience negative symptoms such as withdrawal, feeling flat, lack of function or emotion, apathy and feelings of depression. Whilst I was on a psychiatric ward in the early 1980s, I suffered severe clinical depression during my days as a revolving door patient (an unofficial term for someone who is frequently in and out of hospital). I'm not ashamed to admit that I did not shave or shower much at that time. I had no motivation and "My confidence was in my boots". A briefcase full of money, a glamour model or a celebrity in front of me would not have meant anything to me at that particular time of my life. People would try to motivate me, however, in my burnt out state and depressive existence, all I wanted to do was sleep and eat; I guess this was due to a combination of over sedation, low mood and my overall state of mind.

I am convinced these days that keeping my daily maintenance and routine up has helped me to get to the place I'm now in my life. It has not been a "Bed of roses and no pleasure cruise" getting my act together. It has been hard work and I can reflect now without "Blowing my own trumpet" how much effort I have put in to get myself well again and I would not want to live the illness again.

During the chapters of my life connected to being a psychiatric inpatient I was never prescribed anti-depressants, so I guess I started reflecting on my situation and status during these dark days of my existence. As I have mentioned in my other books, the words positive or recovery never seemed to be discussed during my experience as an inpatient. I commenced to psycho-analyse myself and started to think positively, doing the opposite to "Bad is good and down to up" etc...my thoughts being my words and aspirations. I never really told anybody what I was thinking just in case they thought I was even crazier than I was diagnosed. I looked at myself in the mirror, instead of blaming some of my turbulent times, events

29

and other people. I would reflect back and analyse some of the choices and bad decisions that I made, which had contributed to my downfall and eventual breakdown.

I guess that once you have hit rock bottom, there is only one way to go and that is up, however this is not so easy when you have a severe mental health problem, dysfunctional and you are not in control. "It is a journey not a destination as far as I'm concerned and yeah you can make your own stops" if you catch my drift? So here I'm digressing again, but the point I'm making it's not a case of "Pulling yourself together like a pair of curtains" as I have quoted before, it's not as simple as that. People have different and varied perceptions of how one should be or react. As far as I'm concerned, no one can judge another human being unless they have walked in their shoes. We are all unique in our own sweet way and I believe that the answer is something you do not look for and find; the answer lies within ourselves. Hence the theory you can only help someone who is prepared to help themselves.

**Chapter 4: My Employment**

Two decades after I first became ill, I was in attendance at a service user staff group meeting known as, Beyond the Cuckoo's Nest. It was at this particular meeting that I was told by a health care professional that the government was giving opportunities to people who had experienced mental health problems. This person obviously believed in me and I found out at the meeting that the Rotherham Early Intervention Team (EIT) in Psychosis was recruiting staff to create a new team in 2005. I wasn't successful with my first interview, however another opportunity came six months later and I was successful in securing a post within the Rotherham EIT as a Support, Time and Recovery (STR) worker on the 14th of November 2005. I will always remember the day when I first parked my car on site. I felt like this was my spiritual workplace and that a lot of my stigmas were dissolved as I turned full circle from service user to staff member. I can vouch as the years go on, that I have never been treated any different to any other member of the team and have never felt the sting of stigma in my employment.

The team work in a non-judgemental way and this can only be positive regarding empowerment with our service users. Our team currently works with people between ages 14-35; however the new service model in the NHS has taken off the age cap in some EIT's for people experiencing their first episode of psychosis. Part of the Early Intervention ethos is that the earlier the psychosis is detected, the better the outcome. It's like catching a cold before pneumonia. However, sometimes we do work with people with a long duration of untreated psychosis (DUP) even though it's still classed as their first episode of psychosis. DUP is the time interval between the onset of psychotic symptoms and the course of treatment.

Initially, in my new post, I had to stay in the office for two weeks while I waited for my criminal records bureau (CRB) check to come through. Nevertheless I attended team meetings, however I was anxious to get out of the office and out into the field working with service users. I recall my first visit that I went out on with a Community Psychiatric Nurse (CPN) to see a service user. As I have previously mentioned I couldn't believe she was actually reading him the medication information leaflet about possible side effects and giving him choices if this medication didn't suit him. In my experience as a service user, I was never given this information and straight away it just showed me how much things have changed when a person centred approach is used.

The British Association for the Person-Centred Approach (2013) says a person-centred approach is based on the theory and philosophy of Dr Carl Rogers. It is a non-directive approach that encourages belief in people's potential and ability to make the right choices, known as the actualising tendency. An essential part of this theory is that in a particular psychological environment, the fulfilment of personal potentials includes sociability, the need to be with other human beings and a desire to know and be known by other people. Also it includes being open to experience, being trusting and trustworthy, being curious about the world, being creative and compassionate. Examples of this include meeting in a person's home rather than in a clinical setting, and the person's care plan is tailored to the person's needs.

On reflection some of these approaches, attitudes and awareness's were not around in the early 1980s as I have previously mentioned in my other publications: my autobiography 'Sex, Drugs and Northern Soul' and my sequel 'Stigma Worse than Psychosis'. It was almost baron as far as community support for people with mental health problems and follow-up from being in psychiatric units as far as I was aware of. Another significant improvement is the changes in medication; antipsychotic medications have significantly improved in the last ten years to two different groups: Typical-which is the older drugs and Atypical-which is the newer drugs. Older antipsychotics 'Typical' drugs first appeared in the mid-1950s such as Largactil which I have already mentioned; all block the action of dopamine and produce many side effects such as: stiffness, shakiness, feeling sluggish, slow in thinking, uncomfortable restlessness (akathisia) and problems with your sex life. The newer antipsychotics 'atypical' drugs still block dopamine but less so than the older drugs and also work on different chemical messengers in the brain and many have the same effects as the older drugs (Royal College of Psychiatrists 2013).

Our team starts off using very small dosages of antipsychotic medication when we have taken clients on to our services and implemented them into our care plans. I don't see people suffering from as many side effects as they use to and they can now have a better quality of life such as going to work, attending college, courses and driving. There are some myths about taking medication and driving but if a person is stable for approximately six months they can drive a car but need to let DVLA know. Also, their doctor has to sign a disclaimer to show they are fit and well to drive. Employers are positive about people with disabilities both physical and mental to keep them in employment. The Equality Act 2010 has been helpful in giving people with physical and mental impairments protected rights. This strengthens your rights not to be discriminated against and extends the groups of people who have rights not to be discriminated against. People who belong to these groups have what are called protected characteristics which include: age, disability, race, sex, sexual orientation, religion or belief, marriage or civil partnership, pregnancy and maternity and gender identity and gender reassignment (Citizens Advice Bureau, 2013).

The team does not solely rely on medication but also does psychosocial interventions such as Cognitive Behavioural Therapy (CBT) and Cognitive Analytical Therapy (CAT). There are similarities between these therapies as in that they both offer a limit on the number of sessions, both offer a focus on a limited range of goals and may use similar ways of helping you keep track of your difficulties. Both are collaborative approaches, meaning you work actively with the therapist on your difficulties. CBT is good for disorders such as anxiety, depression, panic, obsessive compulsive disorders, etc. It has specific, research proven ways of working with such clients using different techniques appropriate for their presentation. CAT works more interpersonally on relevant, jointly identified issues by creating a working relationship between the client and therapist (The Association for Cognitive Analytic Therapy 2013).

Part of my mental health problems were triggered by low self-esteem and negative thoughts and perceptions. I feel that challenging the negatives to positives in my journey of recovery has enabled the positives to become a feeling and not just a word. The above therapies are successful approaches and I would recommend these CBT and CAT approaches.

Some people refer to "Emptying your bins", letting go, ventilating, etc. This means talking about your problems, however I find that there is great value after predominately working with young males to encourage people to talk about their feelings and emotions and there are great rewards in doing so. For instance, some of my female friends have told me they find it frustrating when their partners or male associates do not understand them

34

emotionally and when you start to recognise and understand people's emotions; I feel that you form better empathy and connections. I can remember when I was a young lad in my adolescence and hung up about a girl at school and I never told anyone about my feelings.

During the first three years of my treatment as a revolving door patient in and out of hospital, I don't recall any doctors, nurses, or psychiatrists or anyone else for that matter that probed or did any assessment concerning my emotions regarding past relationships or traumas. My inpatient experience in those days seemed to be all about medication and behaviour as far as I was concerned; you had to fit the service the service did not seem to fit you. Again, I can highlight how positive changes in psychiatry and psychology have moved on, such as using a holistic approach where you can find out more about a person's journey and their background. For me, "It's not a case of what is wrong with you; it's a case of what has happened to you".

I have seen a lot of changes over the years, for example, counselling was not around and the psycho-education wasn't there like it is now such as sixth form psychology in schools. In my new life, I do presentations, seminars, workshops, talks and networking to schools, colleges, universities, police training centres, ambulances services and a range of other institutions that require a mental health input. I have still been involved in the service user/staff group 'Beyond the Cuckoo's Nest', from a staff point of view. My employer is very good at letting me be an ambassador for mental health awareness, recovery, reduction of stigma, and mental health drug awareness. I feel as though this has been an integral part of my recovery by talking and writing about my journey which has helped to become an empowering and cathartic experience.

Our team works alongside education to keep individuals with mental health problems in education and enable them to continue their studies and reach their vocational goals. I did not finish my school education off and missed sitting my G.C.S.E's due to the onset of my first episode of psychosis in the last year at school. I was a top set kid in my comprehensive school and unfortunately I never picked my education back up until much later on in life. There were no community mental health teams, workers, or advocates to encourage me to get back into education or college at that time. It was like a desert with no resources to access after I came out of hospital in my late teens, early 20s. I am pleased to say that we have come a long way to empower people to pick up the pieces and reach their goals. I was 40 years of age before I went back to college and I completed my certificate in Mental Health Level 3. I have also gained certificates for IT, Health and Safety, Duel Diagnosis and other qualifications. I continue my professional development by attending mandatory and other courses and I am still enjoying writing books. Our team does encourage and support people with continuing their education as I am a big fan of education and think this is the way forward.

I previously highlighted in my past about stigma and this usually comes from lack of education and right information. I am now pleased to say that this education is implemented in psychology and mental health educational establishments. I am finally proud and not ashamed of coming through my mental illness; people who combat cancer and other physical illness often talk about how well they have done and celebrate a sense of wellbeing. I have gained a lot of respect helping others which has also helped me grow as a person.

The Early Intervention Team is a recovery focussed team consisting of: nurses, social workers, occupational therapists, psychologists, psychiatrists, nutritionist, support, time and recovery workers, administrative staff, and a manager who all bring a range of experience to the service users and work with robust care plans tailored to the service user's needs. I continue to attend mandatory training and have gained professional insight and experience as well as my service user experience, which is still very important, however, when you are working collaboratively with other agencies and attending ward rounds, professional experience is paramount and I feel as though I have a nice balance of these two.

I often reflect as part of personal development through my supervision and in professional meetings and I have always been a good talker but feel as though I have become a better listener. Part of my development and recovery enables me to think if I could do things differently and more positively, thus helping the service user to be more empowered, the bigger picture is everyone has the ability to change, think and behave differently.

I have seen a big shift in the last few years about personal responsibility, which works both ways as I have become more confident as I have grown professionally. I feel as though I have settled down and became an integral part of the team. I also feel it's important to keep your own personality and character. I still have my crazy sense of humour and use some of my positive quotes that my grandfather (God bless his soul) taught me, who was a great philosopher. I often see these quotes on social network sites and in educational institutions. I always try to post something regularly on my social networking site and have had tremendous response and feedback from this.

Furthermore, I feel as though it's important to work closely and collaboratively with the family dynamics and carers as these people often know their son or daughter best and it is part of the psychosocial model. Our team carries out carers assessments which identify the carers needs, to give education and the opportunity for carers to be involved in their son or daughter's care plan. We also hold carers groups, which again have been very successful and instrumental for their loved one's recovery. We also offer peer to peer support to show they are not the only person who is enduring this phenomenon. Our team looks at helping people to budget and we work closely with the benefit agencies to help meet their financial and social needs. My mother or family would have had no help or support in the community when I was enduring mental health problems, when I first got discharged from the mental health unit in the early 1980s. I am glad to say that we have moved on as a society, although I still feel there is a long way to go regarding carers support.

Our team offers a variety of groups such as psycho-education; these courses run for about six weeks to give service users education, help and awareness about their illness which is invaluable to their recovery. Having insight and self-awareness into your illness, for me is instrumental to keeping on the road to recovery. The team also offer cooking and nutrition groups thus allowing service users to gain independence and confidence in their health and wellbeing. I can identify through patient experience that if you have been in hospital for a while and have not made a cup of tea or cooked anything for a few months, your confidence can be quite low in this area. This could be because of negative symptoms, low self-esteem or other mental health issues that may hold you back from completing even the smallest of tasks. Making a cup of tea to some people may seem a spontaneous thing to do, however, for a service user who has been disempowered and out of control, this small step can be essential at the beginning of their recovery from a therapeutic point of view. A cup of tea can lead to a sandwich, and then eventually shifts to more challenging tasks such as shopping, preparing a proper meal, washing up, etc. This produces a sense of achievement when this happens for the first time and creates a sense of wellbeing; I can vouch for these small steps as I was in that position, now I'm known as a good tea masher!

EIT have a variety of physical health groups such as sports and activities, these groups are imperative for their overall physical and mental health wellbeing. Currently, whilst writing this book, Rotherham United (my own town football club) is funding and supporting various activities in partnership with our team. I help facilitate a weekly snooker group that gets well attended and has been going now for over eight years at the time of writing this book. I recall that I used to see a service user who's "Confidence was in his boots", with low self-esteem and was isolating himself in his bedroom. I would visit him in the afternoons initially to see him; at the time he would not engage and was suffering severe psychosis. Then one day I went down to see him and he started to say to me that he liked playing snooker when he was well. This led me to take him on a one to one visit for a game of snooker, where upon, he bought a snooker cue and would just hit the balls without concentrating. Eventually, he was determined to beat me and I could see his motivation coming back to him he started to cue properly and focus on his shots. He took the initiative to phone me up to go to snooker and he would be waiting outside his house upon my arrival with his snooker cue. The EIT have people for three years and this guy ended up back at college and told me that the snooker group helped him to distract himself, gave him a focus and something to look forward to, which helped with his mood and concentration. Later he became an integral part of the snooker group that was formed and the group is still is a success. Eight years later on this group is still well attended, friendships have been formed and other groups have developed from this.

## Chapter 5: Relapse Prevention

A reoccurrence of psychosis is called a relapse and unfortunately many people who have had a first episode of psychosis will experience a relapse in the future. Preventing relapse is essential to recovery.

I was often stubborn and would not seek help or advice when the early warning signs were prominent. I would always try to get myself out of any crisis situation. On reflection, I was in denial and it took me almost a decade to admit that I had a mental health problem. I did not use any coping strategies. I guess I used to soldier on, keep things to myself and use negative escapes as I had mentioned before, for example substance abuse and other antisocial outlets.

Good treatment can help prevent relapse and there are a number of steps you can take that can minimise relapse. These may include: regularly taking your medication as prescribed even when you are no longer experiencing symptoms. I can vouch that I have come off prescribed medication too early when I thought I was ok. I didn't realise that the medication can help keep you balanced, thus preventing an onset of the mental illness. I am pleased to say that there is plenty of education and support about a medication plan that may be tailored to suit the individual. If you feel like your medication is not working or you no longer require it, please seek advice of a medical professional. You would need a phased reduction plan to prevent risk to your wellbeing and physical health. Hopefully this would be in a care plan that would be supervised, monitored, managed with your carers and health care professional.

I feel it is important to get education around your illness and treatment in the recovery process as this helps give insight and better outcomes for the individual affected. I think the better insight you have, the longer you can maintain your wellbeing and quality of life. My friends and family who have stood the test of time and been there for me through the ups and downs have been instrumental of my continuous quest for a fulfilled life.

I have my own stress management techniques which are mentioned in this book and I maintain a healthier lifestyle than in my chaotic past. Some of these strategies will greatly reduce your risk of relapse, however even if you do everything right, the risk of relapse is not completely eliminated and relapse remains unfortunately a possibility. So it is very important to make additional efforts in order to prevent any impending relapse to shorten the duration of any relapses that may occur.

Common triggers for a relapse in psychosis can include family/friend arguments, break up of a relationship, problems with work or school, death of a loved one, drug and/or alcohol use and lack/poor sleep. I again can relate to these issues without getting help and disclosure can manifest in your mind and in your emotional self.

Some common early warning signs would be sleeping too much or too little, feeling anxious or tense, finding it difficult to concentrate, feeling down or sad, feeling high overly excited and elated. You may also be feeling suspicious of others, not taking care of personal hygiene and neglecting oneself. You could with draw from enjoying hobbies or usual fun activities; not wanting to spend time with family and friends, this list is not exhaustive. Sleep deprivation was one of the major triggers to my previous episodes. Prior to being in hospital, I would get thought disordered and ramble on incoherently and nobody would make sense of what I was speaking endlessly about. I lost copious amounts of weight in a very short time and I neglected myself. I could get more and more anxious and even manic and out of thoughts and sorts. I have had grandiose and delusional ideas such as thinking I had special powers. I would also start to feel suspicious and paranoid and I isolated myself from my peers and family. My behaviour and my mood would be noticeable as I could swing rapidly from high to low and my personality became disoriented.

A relapse prevention plan is a good idea that you could make with your family. This individualised plan should be developed when early warning signs are noticed. This plan would outline the steps to contact appropriate service providers. It could initiate stress management or use of medication strategies as appropriate. You should be given a copy of the plan, which could also be part of your care plan. By monitoring early warning signs and taking the appropriate actions, you may be able to prevent a relapse before it occurs. You can periodically review your relapse prevention plan with your support network and you may modify it if needed.

If a relapse occurs it's important to reduce its duration and this will help to improve your chances of good recovery and minimise the disruption to your life. You may identify triggers of relapse, thus giving you a relapse prevention plan and hopefully helping you to gain insight towards avoiding any future relapses.

The following two chapters are written alone by Tina Morgan.

## Chapter 6: Meeting Jason and about myself

I remember first meeting Jason, who is a larger than life character and he also made me feel very welcome to the EIT. I went on many joint visits with Jason and observed that he connects well with service users and was able to relate to them and share his experiences. Jason also listened to the service users and encouraged them to be positive and to never give up. Jason is known for his strong personality and also has a wealth of knowledge about life experiences and mental health. When it comes to being serious he is always there to support people through difficult times, while also being able to put a smile on their face which is essential when going through challenging times. I remember him visiting a service user who was feeling down and he said to him, "Why don't you put on some Elvis Presley music"? Jason loves Elvis Presley and knew that he enjoyed Elvis as well. The service user relaxed and enjoyed the music and his mood seemed to uplift by the time we left his home. The ability to connect to so many different people is not something everyone can do, but when it's done in the right way, it can touch so many people's lives.

The statistics say that mental illness affects one in four people, however that statistic is closing in as so many people I come across have had either their own personal experience with mental ill health, or know someone close to them that had or is experiencing mental health problems. This isn't just psychosis or schizophrenia but also depression, anxiety, bi-polar disorder, borderline personality disorder and many other mental illnesses.

I suffer from generalised anxiety disorder and manage it well for the most part. This means I am still affected by anxiety and able to function well within my work and home environment, however, I have times where I feel quite anxious. I do not tend to come out and tell everyone about this as I have previously mentioned, as I do manage it very well. People whom I am very close to know this, such as my loving and supportive husband James, my mom Louise and sister Dawn. Generalised anxiety disorder (GAD) can be a long-term condition which causes you to feel anxious about a wide range of situations and issues, rather than one specific event. People with GAD feel anxious most days and often struggle to remember the last time they felt relaxed. It can cause both psychological (mental) and physical symptoms which vary from person to person. In Britain it affects 1 in 20 adults (NHS Choices, 2012).

I first experienced GAD in University when I was in my early 20s. I received support from the University medical health team which included my general doctor, psychologist and psychiatrist. They supported me to get through the episode and carry on to succeed in University by completing my Bachelor's degree and eventually my Master's Degree. I also managed well in my own personal and work life by having several jobs at once and spending a lot of time with friends and family.

The second episode, which is still on-going, came after my move to England from the USA. Understandably as one could expect with such a tremendous life change, but it got worse after having my beautiful daughter Sienna Louise. This was due to having a traumatic, unexpected premature childbirth as well as supporting my daughter with surgery three months after she was born due to her having a benign sacral teratoma in her lower back. I am still on the road to recovery from GAD with wonderful support of friends, my close family and most importantly my husband James, I am able to carry on and manage it. I work 34 hours a week, I am a very involved mother and manage a social life. I am not saying it's easy because there are times I would rather just give up, however I find it in myself to not give up and this can be due to various factors such as working in mental health with a wonderful, compassionate team. I have a supportive family and friends, as well as being taught from my mother very young that you never give up, no matter how hard and difficult life can get. Having Sienna has definitely given me strength to never give up.

Finding a balance in life is essential; everyone needs time for themselves even from kids, partners, family, friends, etc. It is paramount to take care of yourself, most importantly, because if that is neglected you will be of no use to anyone else. Work and a personal life balance are so important and sadly, many couples don't always manage this and that is why I feel there are so many breakdowns in marriages as well as abandoned friendships. Nutrition, rest and exercise are equally empowering and this awareness is very important in taking care of yourself, which can help to keep you physically and mentally well. This is easily neglected many times by people and causes a ripple effect when done so. For example, working a lot can lead to minimal sleep, not eating well and then eventually sickness. This is because the body and mind need the right things to keep it running, like a car needing gas (petrol as they say here in the UK), maintenance checks, etc.

When I make the time and the key thing here is make the time, I use relaxation to help with clearing my mind which is important to my overall wellbeing. I find that I feel more relaxed and can think clearly when I have done this. Calming the mind is essential to giving oneself some rest and to minimise stress that occurs in our daily, busy lives. It's important to make the time rather than say we don't have time, as we can always make the time for things that are important. I have done many years of yoga, which I must admit, have not done in over a year due to financial pressures and again, time. I say financial pressures as I feel I get more out of yoga when

47

I attend a yoga class through a yoga centre, but this can be costly and requires a few hours per week. This is not to say it can't be done at home on your own or with a DVD, it's just I prefer to go to a yoga class. When I do yoga, I find it to be very beneficial as well for both the body and mind. I have been trying to practice mindfulness, which is a way of paying attention to the present moment and can use techniques such as meditation, breathing and yoga. It helps people to become more aware of their thoughts and feelings so that they are better able to manage them, instead of being overwhelmed by them.

There are many positives to practising mindfulness such as: boost attention, enabling better concentration, improved relationships, gives more insight into emotions, and help with stress, anxiety, depression and many physical problems as well (Mental Health Foundation, 2013).

I feel recovery is important and it's something one continues to do throughout their life as we all recover from various traumas, events, etc. The most important thing is to look after yourself and find someone or a few people to talk to. There are also plenty of self-help groups available out there for people to find support and to talk about their illness; I encourage people to take advantage of this. It's important to not feel alone and despite everyone having their own unique experience, it's also important to know you are not alone either. I was impressed by Jason's tenacity and his journey overcoming mental illness, so much so that I did an assignment for my Mental Health Certificate Level 3 after reading his books. Some of the following content may reflect on what has been mentioned before as it may have an element of previous disclosure by Jason.

## Chapter 7: Tina's Assignment

I am writing about Jason Tune, a colleague of mine as well as a friend. He was admitted to Rotherham Psychiatric Unit (as it was known then but now called the Mental Health Unit) when he was 16 years old in December 1980 and was given the diagnosis of Manic Depression, now called Bipolar Affective Disorder. Jason had five psychotic episodes and was in and out of the hospital several times. The last two hospital admissions were drug induced psychosis. There was not one specific trigger to Jason becoming mentally unwell but several factors building up which included: having a reputation as a tough guy in the area, turbulence at home, breaking up with a girlfriend, working a man's job while still in school and also an army cadet and his dreams of a military career being shelved, staying out all night drinking and using cannabis.

According to the International Classification of Diseases (ICD) (2013), "Bipolar affective disorder is characterized by two or more episodes in which a patient's mood and activity levels are significantly disturbed, this disturbance consisting on some occasions of an elevation of mood and increased energy and activity (hypomania or mania) and on others of a lowering of mood and decreased energy and activity (depression). Repeated episodes of hypomania or mania are classified as bipolar." Basically, sadness and happiness generally have a direction and meaning; you know where they come from and where they are going. Depression and mania appear hopeless and bottomless and are no longer related to the events that occur around you, you are no longer yourself. Bipolar affective disorder falls within the Mood (affective) disorder classification, which means that the central disturbance is a change in affect or mood to depression (with or without associated anxiety) or to elation and often accompanied by a change in overall level of activity. Most of these disorders tend to be recurrent with the onset of individual episodes related to stressful events or situations.

Other mental health disorders and their definitions according to the ICD include: personality disorders, anxiety disorders, psychotic disorders, substance-related disorders, eating disorders, and cognitive disorders. Personality disorders are deeply ingrained and enduring behaviour patterns, manifesting as uncompromising responses to a wide range of personal and social situations. These represent extreme or significant deviations from the way in which the average individual in a given culture perceives, thinks, feels, and relates to others. Such behaviour patterns tend to be stable and encompass multiple domains of behaviour and psychological functioning.

Anxiety disorders are distress linked with physical symptoms arising from the fight or flight mechanism such as panic, persistent nervousness, sudden onset of palpitations, sweating and various other physical symptoms which may be linked to thinking patterns that reinforce sense of threat or doom.

Psychotic disorders describe an individual who is experiencing things outside what is considered normal within their culture. Delusions, hallucinations, perceptual disturbances, and the severe disruption of ordinary behaviour can occur.

Substance-related disorders include alcohol, various drugs such as depressants, stimulants, painkillers and hallucinogens which may or may not have been prescribed, and tobacco that impact the functioning of the brain.

Eating disorders mainly focus on the anorexia and bulimia category. Anorexia is characterized by deliberate weight loss, induced and sustained by the patient and the focus is on an over concern with body shape and weight. Bulimia is characterized by repeated bouts of overeating and an excessive preoccupation with the control of body weight, leading to a pattern of overeating followed by vomiting or use of purgatives.

Finally, cognitive disorders which involve problems in the functioning of the brain which is characterized by impairment of memory, learning difficulties, and reduced ability to concentrate on a task for more than brief periods.

Jason first noticed when things were not right when he came out of the bathroom at a pub and everything seemed different, then a sudden rush of light, buzzing and disorientation all hit his head. The feeling went from his limbs and the voices of people seemed to be miles away and faces swam into view and disappeared again. Jason described the feeling to when he was five years old and sitting on a fast moving roundabout in a local park. On that night, events and his reactions were random and during the night he would have flash backs of the evening in the pub but every time the running order would be different.

At times Jason would stay up all night with a lot of energy and have grandiose ideas, such as thinking he was psychic and superior to others. Looking back, Jason says "The gateway to mania is through loss of sleep" In his autobiography 'Sex, Drugs and Northern soul'; Jason discussed not having the experience or mental tools on hand to deal with the rejection of his first puppy love. He buried his feelings inside a safe that was hidden in the furthest corner of his mind. He described the toll of the loss of his adolescence knock back, trying to catch up with schoolwork, the disparity of his home life, working long hours and the lack of sleep building up. "I was like a tinderbox ready to go off and it required the smallest of sparks to ignite the igneous vapour in my head" (Brown and Tune, 2006, p.74). Jason's mother always maintained that someone spiked his drink that night at the pub while he went to the toilet and the hospital results stated there were traces of an illegal chemical in his body. "I admit that I was close to a breakdown but the introduction of some unknown chemical tipped the fragile balance between knowing and mental escape" (Brown and Tune, 2006, p.76).

When Jason first received his diagnosis he didn't even know what it meant and had suffered being unwell for many years prior, without being given a diagnosis. There are advantages and disadvantages to receiving a psychiatric diagnosis. The two advantages are access to services and the comfort of having a diagnosis, which can give legitimacy to an individual's experiences. Having access to services is very important for many people, such as a child with autism who needs the right support in place to do well in school. Having a diagnosis can provide people with the right medication and can allow them to do further research into their specific diagnosis which can allow the individual to be more knowledgeable of their illness so they can start to take control. The disadvantages of receiving a psychiatric diagnosis would be the stigma attached to having a mental illness and psychologically institutionalised, which Jason states. Stigma is the label attached to the mental illness and remains on that person's record forever, such as Jason reports having to pay more for his house insurance due to having mental health problems, even though he has not suffered an admission in years. Psychologically institutionalised means suffering from low self-esteem and always second guessing yourself such as when someone asks you how you're doing, you can easily mistake that to mean, are you becoming unwell? It also means the people on the ward become your family and friends, in a sense, your entire world and the label never psychologically leaving you.

"The direct impact of my psychiatric health problems were a significant enough blow without being compounded by the devastating aftermath of the stigma" (Tune and Warburton, 2009 p.12). Stigma affected Jason the most, as he wrote a book on it called 'Stigma Worse than Psychosis'. He also found it difficult getting back into the community as he spent a good portion of his childhood and early adulthood in the hospital. Rehabilitation services, as they are today, were not available at the time when Jason was leaving hospital and going back into the community. Psychologically, Jason felt he couldn't discuss his feelings with his family and friends because he didn't want to burden them and young men on his estate did not share their feelings with others. "The whole business of not being able to discuss my feelings resulted in me becoming isolated on my estate with my family and friends being physically all around me but psychologically a million miles away" (Tune and Warburton, 2009, p. 17). Jason was reluctant and embarrassed to be seen in his social environment but still needed social contact. Jason was socially excluded by his friends, even the lads that talked about being blood brothers and so forth were nowhere to be seen, as well as the army cadets. "Occasionally I would see an old associate who used to be eager to be seen with me at the youth club, or wherever else, when I was top dog on the estate and they would cross the road so as to not have to walk past me" (Tune and Warburton, 2009, p.18). On the positive side, he was able to get onto a smaller ward, under a doctor who gave him the correct diagnosis and medication. Jason started feeling better generally and his mental state improved drastically and he joined the 'back to work' group and eventually his confidence was increased.

Jason's relatives were supportive most times and caring and what they lacked in experience of dealing with mental health, they made up for with love. Jason didn't feel he deserved this love and believed he brought shame upon his family and let everyone down. His mum initially helped him take the correct dosage of medication at the right time, which eventually backfired as she wasn't very well at the time. This resulted in Jason relapsing due to her giving him the incorrect applied medicine and a misunderstanding on her behalf. Jason's youngest sister Samantha would visit him on the ward frequently. She experienced stigma on two incidents in which she was forced to stand her ground while being taunted about his ill health. When Jason was out of hospital, he still visited his grandparents and they always accepted him for who he was. His relationship with his dad got better when he left hospital and they would work out at the gym together.

Jason experienced discrimination on numerous occasions which he details in his book 'Stigma Worse than Psychosis'. One occasion he remembers going to a Pub nearby the hospital and they wouldn't serve him a glass of coke because they knew he was staying in the hospital. Another occasion Jason clearly remembers discrimination in autumn 1981 when he went to seek work by a construction firm to work on a new sewage system and when he walked into the workmen's cabin on their lunch break, he was unprepared for the barrage of humiliating laughter directed towards him.

Jason also describes a clear memory of experiencing the sting of stigma and people's ignorance when a group of patients from the hospital were taken to their local polling station to cast their votes and have their say in how things should be done. He could hear other voters discussing them in an insulting way within hearing distance and said they must have thought Jason and the other patients were too stupid to tell what they were saying or that what they thought simply did not matter. The terms they used were incredibly derogatory and discriminatory, but the general idea came across that they should not be voting and influencing what was going on in their country, phrasing it in an unpleasant and audible way.

There are many models that explain the nature and causes of mental health but I will look at two models in this paper: the Stress Vulnerability Model and Beck's original Cognitive Model. The Stress Vulnerability Model which was first proposed by Zubin and Spring in 1977 and has evolved since but is still a dominant conceptual framework for understanding psychosis. This model acts as a guide to help people from all situations and experiences, understand the relationships between their internal/external stressors and their illness. It is also used to help people recognise their individual warning signs by supporting them to brainstorm and identify stressors, feelings and thoughts that they experienced prior to their episode. Every person has a different vulnerability to become mentally unwell and it's increased if various vulnerability factors come together at once. These factors could include genetic burdens, temperamental factors and traumatic life events; as well as stressful phases of life such as: puberty, marriage, loss of a close relative or friend, pregnancy and various other events. If these burdens coincide with vulnerability and there is insufficient coping mechanisms then there is a tendency a manic or depressive episode can occur (Psychosis-bipolar.com no date). Jason had various factors such as turbulence in his home life, having a reputation as a tough guy, getting a divorce and fighting for rights to his son, several deaths of close relatives and many other factors. He also demonstrated insufficient coping mechanisms by drinking, taking drugs and fighting.

Beck's original Cognitive model (2001) suggests that depressed mood states are accentuated by patterns of thinking that amplify mood shifts. An example would include jumping to negative conclusions or seeing things in all-or-nothing terms. For example Jason was vulnerable to drugs and alcohol as it provided him an opportunity to feel good about himself.

Changes in behaviour may be a cause or a consequence of mood shifts and negative thinking. Cognitive vulnerability to depression arises due to dysfunctional underlying beliefs, such as I'm unlovable, which is activated by life events that have specific meaning for an individual, such as rejection by their mum and dad, or both. Jason was lucky to have received love from his grandparents which kept him well for quite some time. Beck's model suggested that mania was a mirror image of depression and characterised by a positive triad of self, world, future, and positive cognitive distortions. The self is seen as an extremely lovable and powerful, with unlimited potential and attractiveness. The world filled with wonderful opportunities and overly positive experiences and the future with unlimited opportunity and promise. Hyper positive thinking, which is the stream of consciousness, is characterised with positive distortions, such as depression, but in the opposite direction. These can include: jumping to positive conclusions ('I'm a winner'); underestimating risks ('no danger'); minimising problems ('nothing can go wrong'); and overvaluing immediate gratification ('I will do this now').

Currently Jason has been well and in recovery for over 20 years, he works as a Support, Time and Recovery worker for the Early Intervention Team (EIT) in Psychosis in Rotherham. He feels his own recovery has been too powerful to keep to himself and finds that helping others in his job makes it all worthwhile. Jason won the Chairman's Inspirational Award through Rotherham, Doncaster and South Humber (RDASH) health authority in 2006 for special inspiration for his recovery and work with EIT. He has had two books published on his experiences with mental health and is working on a third book about recovery. Jason networks with the media regionally and internationally and has done various interviews. He speaks with Beyond the Cuckoo's Nest, which is a voluntary mental health educational organisation that addresses and challenges ignorance, negative stereotypes and stigma surrounding mental health issues at various workshops, colleges, schools, police training facilities and many others. His son Jason Lee is in his life and he has a good relationship with his partner Sharon and is a homeowner and landlord.

Jason Tune & Tina Morgan

## Chapter 8: Spirituality in Mental Health

Part of my chemical formula is that philosophy, psychology and spirituality are all linked together. This chapter is an overview of some of the preconceived perceptions of people's ideas around spirituality. I can break it down and fit it into my own views of spirituality. I suppose being spiritually aware has been a key part of my recovery and continued discovery. I am not a religious person; nevertheless, I am a spiritual individual. I for one was confused with this misperception; however, since being aware of my inner self as well as my outer self I have become more in tune with my own individual spiritual growth, beliefs and confidence to continue my recovery and beyond. Recently a friend sent me some information around his spiritual beliefs and I will use some of this literature in the following paragraphs as I can resonate with some of my friend's ideology.

Religions are sets of practices and beliefs that have been created based on epiphanies and teachings of prophets, saints, or sages. Most of my spiritual awareness comes from my own mental health recovery and helping other people to be empowered with their own recoveries. Some religions are intended to lead you into the light of spirituality, either by focusing on an outer form of divinity, or on the spiritual presence within yourself, or both. A lot of people have always wondered how I have survived from having a big reputation, from being a gang leader, drug addict, binge drinker and out of control psychotic individual, amongst other characteristics, that were a possible indefinite setback. In my experience which may not be applicable to others, spirituality can relate to your own personal experience and life events.

Spirituality is a complex word, often misunderstood, as its practices may include meditation. I have been interested in meditation since meeting my soul mate Sharon, who I met at the end of December 2010. It transpired that Sharon, my partner has many spiritual interests and she introduced me to relaxation and meditation. I find that meditation has helped me to settle down and I have become more at peace and at one with myself. In my old life I mostly lived in the fast lane and I often had racing thoughts, anxiety and even mania. Sharon initially said I had trouble slowing the mind chatter down and she observed that I had a problem switching off. Some people may find that they need someone to help them with their practice of meditation and relaxation. Other people may find that a group could be beneficial as the individual may find it difficult to meditate on their own and may find it more empowering in a group. People could consider guided meditation which could help you through the meditation process, for example using CDs, music or even attending a Buddhist Centre.

There are other beneficial health factors about meditation and there has been much research that suggests enhanced physical and mental health well-being. Meditation is now part of my contemplation, discovery of my authentic and holistic self of who I really am. Practising mindfulness has given me a better awareness other people's perceptions and emotions and given me more control of myself. I used to have tunnel vision, just bowling down my own line and perhaps was often consumed in my own smoke and bubble. Nowadays, I do not just see things in black and white; I have become more philosophical and see the bigger picture whilst thinking outside of the box with an open mind.

I also feel as though my own recovery has and is too powerful to keep to myself from my own spiritual point of view. This is a continuing part of my hierarchy and pinnacle to my recovery to help share with other people, who have similar afflicted dispositions that I have encountered. Spirituality is simply the discovery of our authentic self without any trimmings or labels, for example it has helped me to fight my own labels and stigmas, and so much so to help others to do the same. Hence one of my own favourite quotes: "It's a human being with problems not a problem human being". Spirituality gives us a rich source of values and a deeper meaning to life, whatever our religion.

I respect all cultures, religions and diversity. I guess some religions and spiritual beliefs can come together. Spirituality highlights qualities such as caring, kindness, compassion, tolerance, service and community, and in its truest sense, so does religion. Where religion is defined by its tradition and teachings, spirituality is defined by what is real in our own experience, arising from an inner search within ourselves, the finding of our own truth. My granddad, God bless his soul, would often say "Person know thy self". I want to have a bit of humour with an anecdotal conversation I had with an acquaintance from the distant past. I bumped into this old friend and he said to me, "I could remember you fighting with bouncers in town and being chaotic and off your head". I replied, "I have got an old life and I've got a new life, I know who I am, now go away and find out who you are". I must have been a lost soul and I guess the Northern Soul part of my autobiography, Sex Drugs and Northern Soul, is not just about the Northern Soul dancing. It could also be about me as a Northern guy with his own spiritual recovery within myself (Northern Soul, Northern Spirit).

Where religion tends to breed separation — my religion versus your religion, my God is the only real God, my ethics are better than yours, etc. My personal view is that it can get like politics, may cause many arguments, debates and does not seem to have any right or wrong answers for me. Spirituality sees all people as equal, and one of my own sayings is: "I am not better or worse than anyone else" and I used to have a bit of an ego and being spiritually aware has made me a more humble person. Ego from a spiritual point of view is 'Edging God Out'! We are not an 'ism' or a label; we are spiritual beings whose purpose is to awaken to our true nature. I feel as if my true nature is to help others and make a contribution to society as a whole. Self-knowledge is one of the main keys to spirituality, hence the common quote "The University of Life". This has given me more emotional intelligence and helped me to continue to challenge the negatives to positives in my mind. My granddad, bless him again, was a great inspiration to me and he used to say "There's two ways to life the wrong way and the right way". First you explore who you think you are, and from there, you can move into a deeper spiritual view of who you 'really' are. I guess that there comes a point in your own recovery where you learn to be your own doctor to some extent and recognise when you're not doing things right, and who you really are. I feel as though I have found my niche, to give psychological love to another human being is a great spiritual way of being.

People are sometimes a lot more spiritual than they realise, I love Mother Nature and I have become more conscious when I am going for walks in the countryside. I take in the skylines, the clouds, the nature of the surroundings, sounds, smells using most of my senses. I can remember when my mother passed away in 1997 from irreversible cancer in St. Luke's Hospice in Sheffield. After my mum's funeral I went to Kenya on a safari and I took in all the natural beauty of the landscapes such as the mountains, natural plains, and wildlife. I said to someone this is no accident how this comes to be and looking back now, I realised this was a turning point of myself being more spiritually aware.

Becoming more spiritually conscious has helped me expand my thinking and belief in myself. I believe the more you connect to the power within yourself, the more you can be free in other areas of your life and more in control and empowered. i.e. "The mind is not in control, you are in control of your mind". Until we truly know ourselves, we have no idea who we really are; we can all become imprisoned within the confine of our own mind and can only find liberty when we find spiritual freedom within ourselves. The more sensitive and intuitive we become, the more we can empathise with other people's thoughts, feeling and actions. Attitude is one of the main keys to spirituality for me, and I am grateful for my wellbeing and recovery.

I recall a conversation when someone once saying that they were so depressed they were contemplating suicide and that they could do with winning the lottery to help elevate the suicidal thoughts. I replied from a spiritual philosophical view, "We have all won the lottery before we are born". The person looked puzzled and asked what do you mean? I said the odds of us being here are a million to one chance, one egg, and one sperm in millions and we got life, it is a gift. Initially the person actually said he did not understand my philosophy, however I saw him again and he said that he had analysed what I had said to him, and he realised how precious life is. He also said he had been wearing blinkers for a long, long time and was now looking at his life from a different and positive perspective.

I am pleased to say there are guidelines on spirituality for staff in acute care services. Recognising a person's spiritual dimension is one of the most vital aspects of care and recovery in mental health. There has been research done at Staffordshire University.

Spiritual well-being, feeling at ease with essential self, happens when people are fulfilling their potential as individuals and as human beings. People can get very deep but it's up to them, I don't get too deep and see it as a sense of happiness and wellbeing. I can remember a newspaper in my hometown doing a feature on me and asked me quite a lot of questions and one of the last questions was: "What is happiness to you?" My answer was, "Peace of mind". For me, being aware of my spirituality has helped to find that peace and contentment.

People who know me have said I am a big guy and to look at me and say that I would not be out of place stood on a nightclub door as a bouncer, however, as big as I am outside I would like to say that I am as big as that inside. I know my heart is in the right place and I have helped a lot of people outside of work and have reached a lot of people from my disclosures, philosophies and interactions. I personally own up and take full responsibility for the mistakes I have made along the way; nevertheless, these experiences have given me a greater narrative, self-awareness and insight. I feel as though I have tipped this balance and the scales back in my favour and I have also gained a lot of respect by caring for and helping people, while being aware of my spirituality and goodness. In my childhood I would run errands for my grandparents, help my mother with shopping and other chores, as she was not always in good health, I sort of lost my way when I got into drugs and other anti-social activities. Digressing back to visiting my mum while she was ill in the hospice, I recall writing letters on behalf of some of the old people who were coming to the end of life's journey, to their loved ones and their families. There was an element of care that was coming out of me that had been suppressed deep into my subconscious self, now I realise this was a stepping stone to my life's purpose of helping others.

## Chapter 9: Developing my own recovery plan and wellness lifestyle

Some of the contents, information, ideas and strategies have been gathered from my research, evidence-based models of recovery and about information from my own recovery. I have liaised with people from around the globe and I find some of the literature from the USA and other countries very helpful in my continuous recovery and empowerment of my wellbeing. This information can be used safely with other health care treatment. I am not going to say that this is applicable for everybody; neither am I going to say I am a messiah and that everybody is going to recover; however I hope that you may take something positive out of this.

Nearly every element of your life such as where you live, the people you live with, your friends and peers, the things you can't do and things you can do, your possessions, your employment, pets, music and colour affect how you feel. If you are concerned about your mental health or the quality of your life you can do various things and make changes in your life. "You could be an 'A' star student or somebody with limited academic skills, it doesn't really matter in the sense that we all have the ability to think and do things in a different way". In this chapter you may think about where you are in your life and the areas that need to be changed to enable you to get on to that road of recovery and discovery!

It's not always easy to create changes and take the actions necessary without support. I always say, "It can start with very small steps", for example if you have been in hospital for several months and you have not made a cup of tea or cooked anything, that first cup of tea you make could lead to washing the cup after, then making yourself a sandwich and that to me is the one degree shift of change from can't to can as I have previously mentioned from personal experience". I recall having negative symptoms in hospital and a suitcase full of money, a gorgeous female model or anything you could imagine would have not made a difference to me as I was so low in my mood and self-esteem and I actually am the person that made that first cup of tea that led to many more positive changes as I have already documented. The turning point from this was when I was laid on my bed on an acute psychiatric ward in the early 1980's I was reflecting when I used to play football with my friends on the local field near my home and I wanted to get out and be with my friends from my neighbourhood and regain my identity. Enough about me for now and I am going to digress back into the action plan.

Every time you take a positive step in creating change in your life, reward yourself and give yourself a pat on the back. When I first took that positive step it led me to take more positive steps and I would buy myself records, which were popular back in the early eighties to reward myself. I have always been a fan of a "Problem shared, is a problem halved" and feel it is nice to have a friend to talk to and spend time with. Keeping a diary may help you plan, get back on track and get organised as I was one of the most disorganised and a chaotic people around; keeping a diary has helped me restructure my daily maintenance. Thus enhancing my well-being and this has helped empower me to write and share my experiences to a wider audience.

Changes can take time and may be difficult as everybody is individual. "Everybody's DNA and fingerprints are all different". You may have to overcome many obstacles. I started by taking very small steps and my advice is to keep trying and don't give up. I know that is easier said than done and I appreciate as I've said before that we are all individuals, we all go at our own pace and move at different stages. Be persistent and keep working at whatever it is that will make you feel better and enjoy your life more. For me making changes is being able to see beyond yourself to what the solution might be, in other words "Feed the problem the problem will grow and feed the solution the solution will grow".

Creating change is something you need to do for yourself as no one else can do it for you. "As you are stuck with you, you cannot be anyone else so you might as well enjoy being you and only you can be you". Others can help to empower and support you to create that change; however it's up to you to do what needs to be done and you will be the one that benefits from successful change.

## Chapter: 10 Personal responsibility and regaining control of your life

At the time of writing this book I am more than 20 years in recovery from a major drug-induced psychotic episode and I feel as though I have control over my own life. I have had a total of five episodes of psychosis from the age of 16, when I had previously been a binge drinker and occasional cannabis smoker and later addicted to amphetamines and using other substances. My mind was fluctuating from reality to mania delusional and grandiose ideation and I have also experienced long periods of negative symptoms and low self-esteem. Anyway, back on to the recovery and discovery.

Taking some control back over your own life, is when you have gotten over the first hurdle and starting to create changes in your circumstances and wellbeing. If you don't feel you have control over your own life, it is essential that you get empowered to take control again. It is very difficult to feel well when you're not in charge of your own life. Tina, who is helping me write this book, is going to ask me the following questions that could have helped me to regain control over my life and affairs. You the reader may hopefully take something out of the following discussion between Tina and me.

*"Do you feel that you have control over your own life these days Jason? And if so, how long have you felt this way"?*

"I feel as though I am in a better place nowadays than I obviously was in my dark times as a mental health service user and drug addict. I am more mature and listen better and have positive influential people in my life, people who believe in me and share some of my views on mental health empowerment and recovery. My family have always been there for me and without their love, which is paramount; I don't think I would have made it to where I am now. I also have a few friends that have stood the test of time, I would like to say I have developed new and more fulfilling, stronger friendships and relationships. I have recently been made aware of three friends of my past who have unfortunately passed away in the last year through drug addictions. I am very lucky to have come through the other side and I recently did a presentation at college on the funeral day of one of my best pals from those days. I reflected and thought to myself that this could have been me, Thankfully, I diverted onto a different path in life to my old friend from the drug scene. As I have previously said one of my granddad's favourite quotes, "There are two roads to life, the right road and the wrong road". I didn't listen to my granddad when I was younger; I now listen to him in my heart. It's not been easy and initially the drug world had been my escape from a lot of turmoil in my life, however I really want to highlight that this was a complete false sense of security.

I have been substance-free for over 2 decades and my mental well-being has got better over the last 20 years. So I guess coming off drugs and being clean has been one of the main turning points for my insights and self-preservation. You can do your maths; it's simple, no drugs for over 20 years and no psychosis for the same period. I feel as though these drugs were the main reasons for my last two drug-induced admissions. I have always been battling bi-polar disorder since I was diagnosed when I was 16. Even now I am still learning coping strategies and better ways of dealing with stress and triggers. I have grown up a lot from my wild days and I have learnt valuable lessons. Writing has also been a liberating experience and has helped me let go of some of the pain and suffering.

I would advise people to talk to someone when they are feeling as though they are not in a good place. When I was a kid there was no education about mental health and well-being. "We have a mental side as well as a physical side" you would be surprised how many people do not realise this. I have asked people from all occupations and walks of life if they were taught this at school and not surprisingly in my experience the answer is they have not. As I said before, I do digress and back to your question Tina, recovery for me is discovery, I have a philosophical approach of reinventing myself and looking at things in different ways. I have moved on and unhitched the trailer, and let go of lots of garbage that was "Living in my head rent free". My sister Cheryl once said, "He gave us eyes to look one way". I do reflect a lot however, as my youngest sister Samantha used to say to me when I was in depression and having negative symptoms, "You have to keep thinking positive". At the time, I used to think, what is she on about? As positivity and recovery was not mentioned in mental health and now it's the norm from day one of meeting somebody who is unwell.

I could talk a lot Tina about my journey and taking control back of my life and hopefully empowering other people who are and have been similarly afflicted like myself, is of course a very empowering thing to do. Nevertheless, as I would say "It takes more than one ingredient to make a good cake". "It's never more than one thing that screws you up and it's never more than one thing that puts it right, everybody needs some support and does not do it on their own". I have come off my soap box a long time ago and it's not just about my experience, I am passionate about the recovery movement and de-stigmatization of mental illness, That is still on going and I hopefully will remain a positive advocate for this movement.

Tina is now asking me *"Do you blame anyone else for being unwell and your negative experiences, the bad decisions and choices you have made in the past on your journey?"*

I must admit in my adolescence I used to blame my mum quite a lot as I did not have a good relationship with her. I now realise my mother had her own issues and did not have an easy life herself. If you the reader feel that I am not disclosing too much about my childhood around my mum, it is that I have learned to forgive and forget and move on and I don't want to talk negative about my mum as I'd like to recall her as a character in many ways, she was there for me when I was a lost soul. As a spiritual person I hope she is smiling down on me and I am sure she would be proud of where my life is now. My mother was a tough cookie and I suppose I would never let anyone push me around or bully me and my physical strength has now transferred to my emotional and mental well-being. As the quote I once heard from my late brother Dave as I have said before "The journey from the head to the heart is the longest and hardest journey of all".

A lot of people in psychology sometimes refer to what happens in childhood as a marker that can determine who you are as an adult. For me, if you have had a hard childhood you can be determined to make your adult life better as I am proof in the pudding. I can remember a psychologist at a conference asking questions after his seminar and I told him that I had not got a question or any answers regarding his presentation and I quoted, "I didn't do anything much before I had a breakdown, however I have done a lot more since and I now see it as a turning point and not a crisis point". In other words, "If you are bowling down a line that is not working out, you obviously need to re-discover yourself and bowl down another line".

In my opinion it's no good having regrets or blaming other people as I take full responsibility for my actions and mistakes. I was the person who took drugs; no one sat on top of me and forced me to take drugs. I do not blame getting in the wrong crowd, because there were times, I am not proud to say that I was probably the leader. "There is no saint who has not been a sinner". I used to feel a bit sorry for myself and look for excuses and blame and counter blame would be on the agenda. I came to a stage in my life, which you can see on my You Tube video on stigma that I had filmed in 2010 www.youtube.com/watch?v=917qVjwuaDs, highlighting that I was not doing things right in my life, I had to look in the mirror and take a long, hard look at myself and think could I think in a different way? Could I do things in a different way? And could I take more personal responsibility for my affairs and my life? The worst thing that could have ever happened to me is that I could have looked back and wasted my life. I obviously empathise with a lot of people who are suffering mental health problems and other issues that could be a permanent set-back for them. I guess that empathy will always be one of my main strengths and tools to use in my working and social life. In the face of adversity, I feel as though I have tipped the scales favourably for myself and now live a more complete and balanced life.

*Tina says, "After I read your autobiography, "Sex, Drugs and Northern Soul" it seems that true love has eluded you and has anything changed"?*

Yes Tina I do agree, I guess when I look back analyse and reflect on my life. Reading back through my autobiography I can see the decisions, the pitfalls, the ups and downs, chaotic lifestyle and my illness. I suppose I was always searching for something and it took me years to realise that the answer was mainly in myself. As the quote goes, "You have to learn to love yourself before you actually love someone else". From my point of view, is that how would I perceive love if I didn't know what it was. Jimmy Ruffin once said in a song, "A man without love he walks in the dark". I suppose I can relate to it as well, I have said before I was a lost soul and a rebel without a cause. Love to me is paramount in my new life and I find it difficult at times to connect with people who are not caring, have not got a compassionate nature and a humanitarian attitude to others. In my mental conscience I have an approach, attitude and awareness philosophy and I call this the 3 A's. One of my philosophies is about communication, love and respect "Anything that goes right is about good communication and anything that goes wrong is about bad communication".  Good communication with my partner is vital to our mental and emotional side of our love and relationship.

Sharon, Jason's partner is just telling me (Tina) now from her perspective that Jason is a kind, thoughtful, loving person. Sharon says one of Jason's qualities is that he loves very deeply and she doesn't have to question his love. Jason is very forthcoming with his feelings and emotions and has a massive sense of humour with his love. Jason has a lot of female friends who tell him that they find it frustrating that their partners or spouses don't understand them emotionally. It's no surprise that Jason has got more female friends than male friends, his sisters have also helped him to channel his emotions and express himself freely. Talking freely about your feelings is a real strength for him and not a weakness. Jason often jokes, "Having all these sisters, means I have never won an argument in my life". Jason has a zest for life and has wonderful energy, which at times is a bit overwhelming but I would not be without his presence and his love in my life. Jason doesn't put restrictions or boundaries on our relationship. I often joke back with Jason that we are both free spirits in our relationship and we know that we have different ideas, perceptions, interests, hobbies and outlooks on life. The word respect is always paramount above all and I feel respect is an anecdote of love. *Tina says, "Thank you Sharon for that information".*

*Tina is now asking is there any response to what Sharon has just said?*

I will now give an overview of my love regarding Sharon and general appreciation of life. In 2010 a colleague at work asked me between the Christmas and New Year period what I was doing for the New Year; I jokingly said, "When you least expect something, it usually happens", this is the period when I met Sharon. Sharon had requested my friendship on Facebook and I accepted her request being the gentleman that I am. I have always been partial to a good looking blonde! Joke apart, Sharon had remembered me from my late teens and had read my autobiography on a holiday. She also went to the same school as me and I guess it was sort of turning full circle for both of us albeit from different perspectives. She had been living out of the area for most of her adult life and had returned to the catchment area near our school due to circumstances. I was settled in my own home as well not too far away from Sharon. We talked over the phone for a few days and I could not wait to speak to her when I came in from work after my tea. We had so much in common she even made me laugh about my mother saying something complementary about her.

The bond between us was almost static and we hit it off immediately. Our first date was on New Year's Eve and I introduced her to some of my family at a cousin's New Year's Eve party. My family immediately took a liking to Sharon and my dad said she is the best woman that he has ever seen me with. My sister Marina and other sisters Cheryl and Samantha agree. Sharon and I have many similar interests and we both like holistic and alternative therapies, Sharon also works in the NHS as a health care worker. We have a slightly different contrast as she works for physical health and I work in mental health, although we are both hopefully empowering people. Love to me is a power and strength and the foundation to a fulfilling relationship and happiness. I would rather be on my own than to be going through the motions and living a false life. I still love Northern Soul music and often joke, "All good things come from the soul".

Sorry guys I am now going to rewind back to the late 70s early 80s when I left school prematurely to go on my mental health inpatient venture. One of the setbacks after my onset of acute psychosis was that I did not finish my exams and G.C.S.Es at school. I did not have any qualifications to fall back onto and had no references from education. I now help people to get back into work and education and pick up the pieces in their life, which I find instrumental and essential as part of their recovery. I am glad to say that my team mates adapt this philosophy as part of sharing optimism and recovery. I enjoyed my college courses for my current post and felt that since I have been back into education, I have opened up to more learning and have a zest for enhancing my skills and professional development. As I say I left school with no qualifications due to my first mental breakdown; I now have several qualifications and I am involved in other on-going educational programmes regarding mental health recovery and empowerment for my job specifications. I also have new hobbies, for example I am enjoying spiritual awareness meetings outside of work with Sharon and we have met a lot of like-minded people who link with these feelings and philosophies. As I have previously mentioned, to give 'psychological love to another human being is a great niche'.

In my day job, I often help people to get organised with their finances and help support people regarding their housing situation. I recall prior to my last admission in hospital that I nearly lost my tenancy; I had a lot of red letters, outstanding bills and debts. This contributed amongst other things to my stress and decline of my mental health. I have different ways of managing stress and have developed my own coping mechanisms nowadays. For instance, I am using an analogy as follows: I see stress sometimes like a cluttered clothes cupboard that may be full of clothes and the clothes may all fall onto the floor when you open the cupboard door. This analogy continues when you sort the clothes out, putting them in neat piles and placing them back into cupboards. This is a step by step easy way of explaining how to regain control of your emotions and stress. I will use more examples as we go along.

One of the best forms of coping and maintaining a healthy level of mental wellbeing is by developing a good range of coping strategies. You can't always change your situation but can change the way you perceive and react to it. As I said before, "Feed the problem, the problem will grow and feed the solution, the solution will grow". When you are not doing well, it is usually through a pattern of negative coping strategies and negative experiences. Sometimes when we are desperate to cope with stress, we may use strategies that seem to help in the short term but may make us feel worse in the long term. These can include: avoidance, use of substances or harming and neglecting ourselves in some way. However, the focus on this book is about challenging the negatives to positives and the optimism of recovery and beyond. Discovering coping mechanisms is something that I was not aware of in my naivety and early life. I used to just carry on regardless, without realising that I needed to protect my well-being. I recall having a broken leg when I was a steel erector and I started putting all my

77

weight on my strong side in my recovery and I would take my time climbing up ladders instead of rushing up like I had done prior to breaking my leg. I would also have my tools in my tool belt on the opposite side of my weakened leg to help to keep the strain and weight off my healing leg. I guess I was learning coping mechanisms for my physical health problem. It can be similar if you have never had a mental health problem; you could just go about life without worrying about protecting your mental well-being, like I did. Anyway after my break down and gaining insight I developed some coping ideas so that I would hopefully not relapse again.

Here is a general list of coping strategies that you may find helpful from my general toolbox. If I am stressed I talk to my partner and vice versa. I can talk to other colleagues at work; I have management supervision and group discussions with my other colleagues. I go to the gym for half an hour of cardio each morning and do swimming at other times and have longer sessions over the weekends. I practise a lot of relaxation, meditation and mindfulness as illustrated before, as this helps combat my stress and helps to keep me balanced. I find that writing has been a relief of strong suppressed emotions and a real powerful experience; you may find that you might want to write your thoughts and feelings in a notebook. As previously stated, I used to be very chaotic and disorganised; for the best part these days, I would like to say that I am organised, punctual and assertive. I am now eating healthier and exercise regularly and this helps balance my equal Librium in my favour for my overall wellbeing.

I now listen to advice, whereas I used to reject it and felt it was a weakness to talk about my emotions or feelings and would think people would not understand anyway. So sharing my ideas and perceptions has made me grow as a person. Sleep deprivation was one of the major triggers to my mental breakdowns and I am now in a better routine with sleep and this helps balance the equation for me rather than against me. I take time off from home and work responsibilities and have days out in the countryside and consciously plan a holiday abroad annually. I like to make plans ahead as this keeps me focused, challenged, thus preventing me from being bored, mundane, looking back and living in the past. I would definitely take medication if I was ill alongside the medical advice, making sure I get my medication checked regularly and get a second opinion if in doubt. I personally like support groups, these groups can be very therapeutic and beneficial for certain individuals. I have been involved in several service user, ex-service user and professional groups on my journey. Again, if you have problems talk to someone or even a counsellor, I have heard of helplines which are helpful for certain people; however I have not used them or implemented them in my experience. Often I would talk to my dad and family on the telephone when I was single and found this very helpful in releasing my stress. Nowadays, I continue to surround myself with positive, affirming, and loving people. Looking good is feeling good, I like wearing nice clothes, presenting myself clean-shaven and I suppose I take after my late-mother with my teeth as I like to keep them polished and always keep my dental appointments. I also like to go on computers researching information, whilst looking at different websites; I love learning something new every day and I also enjoy some of the social sites such as Facebook. Sometimes we don't reward ourselves enough and I sometimes make a list of my accomplishments that I am proud of and have now achieved. I have a wealth of experience which I find invaluable regarding the mental health experience, albeit from a personal or professional perspective. You may want to write things down that make you feel good about yourself. People have often said that I have a good sense of humour and would like to think that most of my energy is positive, doing things that make me laugh and I like to put a smile on other people's faces.

One of my psychiatrists actually encouraged me to keep my humour up and he said that they would never want to take that off of me, it's often been said that I am a character and a one-off. When I was in a bad place and not coping very well, I think I was consumed in my own smoke with my problems and situations were often over whelming and stressing me out. 'Helping others has helped the smoke blow away and I try my best to keep my head clear from negative vibes. I try to do something positive every day, even if it's a small thing like polishing my shoes. In my opinion, "Cleanliness is next to godliness and I like to keep in the spirit of life" nowadays. I use a lot of positive affirmations and quotes which obviously I implement in my books. You may want to distract yourself from something negative or mundane by simply changing the episode of thought and take a nice hot, relaxing bath (whatever floats your boat). I love to listen and dance to music, I also sing and have been told that I don't do a bad Elvis impersonation (however, don't quote me as I now have no hair!).

People who know me and my personality would say that I am bright, cheerful and talkative, "I have been accused of a lot of things in my life, but never boring". I can be opinionative, but respect other people's views and perceptions and hopefully help people channel their ideas into a positive, creative, empowering, logical way. I am very outgoing and can be boisterous and a bit of a chatterbox in a nice way. People say I have a load of energy and enthusiasm. I am passionate about raising positive awareness, challenging the stereotypes and bigotry perceptions of people's ignorance. I remain an activist in the recovery movement of mental health and the reduction of stigma, for the most part of my life, I am content and happy. I like people and socialising with like-minded people. I love traveling and meeting new people and I am assertive and class myself as strong-minded. My experiences overall have made me a better person, I didn't feel as though I had done a lot to help people before I had a breakdown, I used to take life for granted and I guess my narrative on reflection was very shallow in my old life. "It's nice to be important, however it's more important to be nice" I heard somewhere and this saying resonates well within me.

A lot of people in education learn about a lot of subjects but do they really learn about themselves? In my future, I would like to make more educational video diaries, do more presentations in schools and networking to other various organisations and institutions. I hopefully will be promoting mental health wellbeing and education on how to protect your mental side as well as your physical side and disempowering the stigma along the way. After all, we are given physical education from the word go at school and I wonder outside sixth form psychology, how many people have been made aware of looking after their mental wellbeing.

I often come across people in my working life who are not registered with a General Practitioner (GP) or even a Dentist. After all, looking better is feeling better, as we all have a duty to look after our own wellbeing in general. You would be surprised how many people do not know how many services and agencies are out there to help. While it may be hard to get good healthcare it's worth making the effort to get the help you deserve for yourself. I recall when there were hardly any mental health community teams around and it was almost like being on a different planet to what it's like now as far as care in the community is concerned. I advise anybody who has got any distress or know anyone to contact a GP or advisor at the doctor's surgery.

Do you get good health care for yourself?

Do you have a GP or a team of health care professionals who know you and your life circumstances? Can they provide you with valuable assistance in monitoring your health-giving you advice on treatment, providing treatment when necessary and referring you to other health care providers when necessary?

What could you do to ensure that you take good health care for yourself?

Do you get a complete physical health check-up every year?

Even though I have been in recovery for over 20 years at the time of writing this book, I still get my yearly health checks at my GP. It's nice to know that I still have support from my doctors and nurses at my own doctor's practice.

If you are not doing anything about your problems, what could you do to make this happen?

Go for an appointment with a list of any medication that you may be taking or mention what illicit drugs you may be using, give a history of your illness, that of close family members and any symptoms you have any concerns about. Don't think anything is too trivial; the mildest symptoms might give your health care provider clues to provide you with good treatment. See your health care professional if your condition worsens or changes. Don't be satisfied with the outcome of your visit until all your questions have been answered and you feel comfortable with the answers and the suggested treatment plan. If necessary, arrange follow up visits and if treatment is recommended follow your treatment up.

## Chapter 11: Changing my lifestyle around

I remember my dad saying to me that I needed to change my lifestyle around completely after my last discharge from hospital on the 10th of December 1993. I wasn't sure what he meant totally at the time; however I can now reflect and agree that is exactly what I needed to do. I can recall thinking about my life and imagining two wastepaper bins in a kid's classroom, labelling them good and bad. At the time of admission and crisis of this hospital stay, I had been totally out of control and on amphetamines, experiencing drug-induced psychosis. The bad side of the bin was nearly full and there seemed to be very little in the good side. I would think of all the drug associates in the bad side and all the negatives that I had unwittingly disempowered myself with. I could blame getting in with the wrong crowd, etc... however, I take full responsibility. I was part of the wrong crowd, no body sat on me and forced me to take drugs, or implemented the other antisocial choices on me that I had made, as well as the chaotic lifestyle that I had ignited myself into.

On a night time when I was getting ready to settle down, I would take one negative out of the negative bin and cognitively input something positive in the good bin. If over a period of time you had a positive test tube and you injected positivity into a negative test tube you would start to dilute the negativity and break it up and hopefully positivity would become a feeling and not just a word. You the reader may think this is a bit deep, I just want to highlight that we can all think and do things in a different way and that one degree shift of changing this process can lead to empowerment, recovery and the new you!

The drug scene, in my opinion was the major thorn in my side that was holding me back from having a good mental well-being. In my experience, it's been the same for over the last three decades that I have not been aware of many people from the drug scene visiting their peers who are in mental institutions. I sometimes used to visit some of these people off the drug scene when they were a guest of the Queen, (in Her Majesty's Prison). This is one example of many that I could give that shows that being on drugs is an illusion and being around its associations can lead you to think that this is the right way to be; however in my experience this could not be more further from the truth. I must have been delusional at the time, as I now clearly know for me and others who have been similarly afflicted that are now substance abstinent and clean, as a false sense of security.

In my new life I often joke that my "Own buzz is my best buzz" actually it always has been! I will now digress and pick up the drug recovery later on and some of my philosophies and strategies that I implement to help others.

Some other suggestions you may consider about changing your lifestyle, for example if you have never taken drugs, could be around doing too much every day, not switching off properly and not having enough breaks and quality 'me' time. I often used to run around and get nowhere fast, in my manic days. I suppose in the modern world a lot of us may feel that there are not enough hours in the day to achieve everything we want to do. My strategy for this phenomenon is that we can only live the day we're in. I remember an old TV advert when I was a kid, that use to say "A Mars a day helps you work, rest and play" I now know what that means without the chocolate Mars bar, as I am currently on a healthy eating plan. I have previously mentioned before, my partner and I practice relaxation and meditation and I feel that this helps me unwind as I have always had brain chatter and racing thoughts. I now practice mindfulness and being at one with myself. I have got loads of ideas, a few projects on the go and even a couple more books to write, however I know for me that I have to finish one thing at a time off and I don't "Put my hands into too many pies".

My partner Sharon has just told me that one of her coping strategies to stress is to remove herself from the situation that is causing the anxiety. She said this is not always doable but being mindful can help.

Over lunch with Tina and Sharon, I mentioned a lot about personal awareness, mindfulness, self-preservation and protecting one's self. I have always put others before myself and often "Wore my heart on my sleeve". I had been subconsciously wearing a lot of people's sensitivities and disappointments and at times failures. This can lead to feeling depleted of your own positivity and energy. Hence the terminology, "Some people are like energy vampires, they suck all the energy out of you". I have often tried to please too many people with my enthusiasm and goodwill; this has occasionally backfired on me and left me feeling bewildered and not valued. However, in my recovery I recall the last thing I ever said to my psychiatrist before I was discharged, was that I have learned to not be too disappointed when things don't work out as planned. I guess coping with disappointments and setbacks is for me part of my on-going recovery and discovery. What would often take me three or four days to get over, now takes three or four hours and it's reducing all the time. I try not to let things get me down and "I only accommodate people that are in my corner"

I still have quick reactions and I would say I sometimes am spontaneous without being mindful, as nobody's perfect. I don't want to offend anybody with the following quote, "The last person that was perfect was crucified". I think as a society we are all trying to be too perfect and I must say I am not a fan of the politically correct jargon and I say it as it is. I know Tina, who is helping me put this book together, is a big fan of education and an even bigger fan of hearing and saying it as it is, without of course, offending anyone.

Sharon, my partner just chipped in again, saying that people sometimes try to live up to other people's expectations and standards. For instance this can cover sexual orientation, spiritual beliefs that don't fit into your friends and family's expectations; it's about living up to your own beliefs. I don't do stereotyping and I am non-judgemental to the best of my self-awareness. In my experience I find that people have double standards and as my late mother used to say, "People in glass houses should not throw stones". Just so people are not getting confused; Tina my co-writer, friend and colleague from Rotherham Early Intervention Team in Psychosis is involved in a three-way conversation with my partner Sharon and me in our front-room at 2pm on Sunday 23[th] March 2014.

Tina just asked me a question, "Where do you want to go next"? I said, "Running around like a chicken with its head cut off" is not good for an overactive personality and someone who is prone to anxiety and other disorders. I do believe that as a teenager I did not have or know about coping mechanisms, it was just a case of survival and getting on with it. If you are rushing around from one thing to another, you are not really processing the feeling, or experiencing the conscious self and being in the here and now properly or appreciating what we are given for free. One of the things I thought about and have actually used with my peers is that life is precious and is a gift and it goes quick enough without wanting to make it go any quicker.

On reflection, I recall being that far ahead of myself inevitably; I would eventually fall over myself. I now focus better and take one day at a time, "After all you can only live the day that you're in". As I have said before, I practice meditation with my partner and

86

relaxation, for approximately 15-20 minutes a day. I implement this in my daily maintenance to help keep myself relaxed and hopefully enabling me to "Keep my head below the bullets and my knees above the crap", "Not too high and not low". I guess hopefully I'm in the middle now and living more of a balanced life.

You the reader may be thinking why I haven't mentioned medication much. I do believe that medication has its place in the acute phase of psychosis and other mental disorders and illnesses; however I see medication as part of a toolbox and the ethos of my recovery has been aided with the help of medication, other therapies and some of my own philosophies and discoveries. I have learnt for the most part to channel my energy into more positive and realistic ideas. At one time I used to get my hands into that many different projects; I would eventually overwhelm myself and make myself ill with anxiety, eventually mania and then burnout. I would crash and be in a depression, sometimes for several months or longer. Anyway back to the here and now, I do try to finish off any projects or work that I start, I need to keep busy and active; otherwise I am prone to getting bored and even depressed. I guess most people would agree that they would be the same if they were not stimulated properly. However when you gain insight, you start to recognise triggers around negativity and stress, it gives you more confidence and the feeling of being in control and strength to cope with your emotions and life events that crop up for all of us. I guess learning to not get too disappointed when things don't work as planned is an on-going process in my recovery as previously stated; hence one of my favourite sayings that my partner Sharon likes, "If it's meant to be, it won't pass you by". That could be with a job, relationship, a house, car, an opportunity, etc. I don't watch too much TV as I like engaging my brain more into reading, exercise, going for walks within Mother

Nature and taking in my surroundings such as the landscapes, the smells of the flowers and plants and fresh air, the sounds of nature and the sunlight. There is more awareness of the benefits of vitamin D from the sunlight which helps your mood and promotes your overall wellbeing. I guess my story is sort of coming "Out of the shadows into the sun"!

I like to have positive escapes these days, I have illustrated in the past that I have had many negative escapes that could have permanently held me back, for example the money that I use to waste on substances I now use for my holidays and breaks. For instance spending £10 on drugs a week is over £500 per year, you could go abroad and see some of the world and different cultures instead of wasting your money. In my recovery I have experienced some fantastic holidays, countries and a variety of different cultures; going abroad has opened my eyes beyond the narrow mindedness that I was entrenched in. Traveling has broadened my narrative and after my mother had just passed away in 1997, I decided to go to Kenya, which was something that I would have only dreamed about in my chaotic days, when I was ill and I could not see beyond my immediate existence. When the aircraft was flying over Mount Kilimanjaro, my geography days at Kimberworth Comprehensive School in the 1970's came into my memories, I probably learned more in two weeks traveling and experiencing a part of Africa than I did in two years on my coursework. In other words, don't talk about it, get on with it. If you think you can do something, go out and do it! When I was in Kenya, I sort of had a spiritual feeling that all the animals in the wild and on safari were there for a reason, the purple headed mountains, the Indian Ocean, wonderful people. I felt at the time that this is no accident that all this amazing wilderness, wild life and landscape that blend together, is not just science and here for a reason. I recall saying to my mother in St. Luke's Hospice in Sheffield, when she was dying of cancer, on the patio overlooking the grounds that this is like the Garden of Eden, I guess I was preparing her for her passing in my own way.

There was a time I was lost and consumed in my own smoke, helping other people has also helped me grow as a person. Some people have commented and said it's like a "Poacher turning game keeper" since I have become employed as a mental health worker. Prior to me becoming ill I wanted to be a soldier when I left school, as I had previously been a keen army cadet in my teens. I had enjoyed a snapshot of the military as I loved to go to the army camps and engaged in other cadet issues. I loved my uniform and experience; however, this career did not materialise due to my breakdown and being hospitalised whilst in my last year at school at the age of 16. I was disempowered from pursuing a military career and it took me awhile to get well enough to get into full time work.

I became an industrial dismantler and a steel erector before coming back into mental health, as a healthcare professional. At the time that I became a steel erector and industrial dismantler, I never had to disclose that I had previous mental health problems. I would often work away from home, I never needed to mention it to anybody and I could leave it all behind. It was a positive escape for me, it gave me confidence and sense of wellbeing and purpose that I had not experienced before. On reflection this was a very positive period of my life, I still had underlying issues that I had not addressed. I was still running away and looking to put things in the way of my problems. For me, writing has been an empowering experience and it has been a way of letting go of some of my pain and "emptying my bins" which has helped me to grow as a person and give me credibility and challenging the stigmas that mental illness carries.

Since being in my current role as a mental health worker I have become proud, I am not ashamed and do not feel stigmatised as part of my recovery has been to challenge my own stigma and perceptions from others. Hence, "I only accommodate those in my corner" as I have previously quoted. People are proud of coming through their physical illnesses, for example "My cancer's in remission" and "I have got over my pneumonia", etc. So why can't I be proud of my own recovery and what have I got to be ashamed of? The credibility that I have since writing my second book on stigma has given me another niche. I have an extended role and it is on-going working with other agencies and partnerships to raise the awareness and challenge the stigmas unfortunately associated with mental health.

In my job role I meet people all the time who are disempowered and have negative perceptions and experiences. I think one of my best attributes is my ability to believe in people who are going through a difficult time in their life. The first thing I do is to accept people for who they are in a non-judgemental way. As the saying goes, "Don't judge anyone unless you have walked a mile in their shoes". I have a built in approach, attitude and awareness philosophy and I find this empathy invaluable in practice. As a patient I could sense who was kind and who cared. I empathise and try my best to keep things on a level of equality, my values, principles are respected and I have reached a lot of people locally, nationally, internationally and for the most part stay grounded.

I love my job and as I have said before, I feel as though my own recovery would have been wasted had I not used the positives to help others. People have said that I have personal experience which is invaluable when empowering others with similar dispositions. Of course I would be lying if I said that my experiences haven't helped others. In my professional capacity, I work collaboratively with other agencies and I attend ward meetings, caseload meetings and I have developed a professional language and understanding of the dynamics in my multidisciplinary team. I went to college to do my certificates and exams. I have mandatory training for a range of topics that the job specification requires. Considering that I left school in 1980 with no exams due to illness, this is my third book. I went to college at the age of 40; I have passed many exams, and gained qualifications and I have a zest for education, giving the right information to grow as a person and to inform others. I am proud of winning an innovative award in my employment and being shortlisted for national and international recognitions.

## Chapter 12: My Drawer Theory

There are a number of stress vulnerable models around; I've seen the bucket theory mentioned in work and on courses/training. I must say I am very favourable of a lot of these models and can relate and empathise with many of the theories. However, I have got one or two strategies and analogies myself. I occasionally visualise and imagine a set of drawers with all the drawers open. That for me is when stress is at its most critical point. Obviously the prevention better than cure philosophy is hopefully to make sure all the drawers do not open. However, I am going to illustrate in no particular order how this drawer theory may help. I recall having red letters and lots and lots of debt before my last admission in hospital and shutting that drawer and getting back in control with my finances was a major turning point from me being chaotic towards being organised. I now encourage people either to see a financial advisor or a debt counsellor to help them work through a budgeting plan. They may let someone else whom they can trust take the reins while they financially feel stable, empowered, then you can close this drawer and take control and reduce the financial burdens.

At the time, I also had relationship problems and was not seeing my son, which was another drawer that was open and was triggering me emotionally and I was going about life in lots of negative ways. I addressed this situation by getting a new solicitor, forging closer links and building trust up with my son's grandparents, after getting myself straight and abstinent off substances and I had a professional key worker who encouraged me to talk about my emotional affairs.

I also recall not being happy with my housing situation and was not living in the area close to my roots or my friends and I felt isolated and disempowered, as the old saying goes, "A Englishman's home is his castle". I moved house and upped sticks that many times in my past, I didn't know whether I was coming or going. It's fair to say that I was chaotic and unsettled for a big chunk of my previous life. It's very important to be happy where you live. I am now pleased to say that I am settled, I am living back near my roots, I have finally got peace of mind and that drawer is locked and I feel secure. I shut that drawer by actually getting support to move from my key worker on discharge into the community.

Another drawer that was open was that I got a lot of emotional problems at the time and I was psychologically addicted to drugs and was in denial. Obviously this denial and negative escapism had a major impact on my overall well-being and consequently was a major trigger to my last episode of mental health problems and psychosis. For the first time ever, I realised I had a mental health problem and an addiction. I started following my treatment up and kept my appointments, I basically played the game, I started seeing things from a different angle and realised the professionals were there to help. I guess they learned quite a lot from my experiences as well, this had been a major drawer to close for me.

I think another stress and a drawer that was ajar at the time, was the people I associated with. I don't mean any disrespect to people who were on drugs or have taken drugs because we all have got our own stories; however I was very vulnerable after coming out of hospital after being a revolving door patient for nearly three years and being in halfway houses, lodges and hostels for another two years. I wanted to break the chains of a mental health stigma and to just be accepted. As I said many, many times to people who have heard me give advice out, I don't blame anyone else for getting me into drugs as that was an informed choice and no one forced me or sat on top of me to take drugs. Looking back I was naïve and wanted to be back with friends outside of the mental health scene. A lot of people had seen me as a big tough guy, my family have often said that I am very sensitive and have a lot of feelings and empathy for others. This is a positive in many ways in my new life and I have learnt to protect myself and detach sometimes emotionally and look at things more objectively and professionally.

There was peer pressure, whilst I was still under the hospital as an outpatient, when I was 19 and working on a car wash project at the time. I have been living on my own in a house that was funded by a mental health charity and suddenly I bumped into two guys that were on amphetamines from the estate that I have grown up on. One was 8 years older and the other was 4 years older than me, they asked me if they could come around to my house. I felt really pleased to be accepted and we shared anecdotal memories of our lives in and around our catchment area. After a while these guys asked if it was okay to do some drugs, initially I was really scared and worried. These guys just got drugs together as if it was nothing and said this will help a lot more than what the hospital has been giving you. I closed my eyes and stuck my arm out, the next thing I know, I had allowed myself to be injected with amphetamines. The rush that I experienced was probably not to be experienced again and I was chasing the first hit and became addicted in due course. The drug scene for me had become an escape and a false sense of security. This has been a major drawer that I have slammed behind me and thank God I can use this experience to help and inform others.

Another wide open drawer that I have evolved from and slowly closed is empowering myself psychologically and emotionally in my adult life, thus coming to terms with my childhood and adolescence.

I don't want to open this up too much as I don't want to talk about my family issues at home in detail; however I have emptied most of my bins from my past and moved on. I have learned forgiveness as well and I have talked to my family and professionals and close friends about my past issues. People say they "Forgive but they don't forget", for me the part of forgive has been erased from their memory; however the part of forget is still there. "I would rather say forgiving and forgetting is not going soft, it is called letting go". Furthermore, I would like to mention that I have unhitched the trailer and let go and emptied most of my bins and as I said before, "Nothing lives in my mind rent free and the landlord has not been around for any arrears". Writing things down, the positive thinking, keeping myself and my wellbeing in check, has given my confidence to inform and help others, which for me feels as though I have not wasted my experiences and actually find this invaluable and empowering.

Another drawer that I found difficult to close and I don't think you ever forget the people who you have loved that have passed away. I am sure if my loved ones could pass me a message from the other side, they wouldn't want me to break down or go to pieces. I guess that is exactly what my message would be from the other side to my loved ones who are still living their lives. There are many different coping mechanisms to many different scenarios and I hope that people can take something out of my philosophies and ideas so far in this book. My objectives are to give hope to people who are struggling and coming to terms with difficulties. I also want to give insight to professionals, students, teachers, parents, peers, law enforcement, etc. That recovery from a life blighted by severe mental illness, addiction and other issues that could be a permanent set-back, is recoverable and possible

I think one of the last drawers I closed was being re-united with my son; I had not seen him since he was 2 years of age until he was age 16. I never missed an appointment with the court welfare officer regarding my son's indirect contact. I liaised with his grandparents on a regular basis during this absence period of fatherhood. This was a very, very long journey for me and I was determined that I was going to be as well as I could be, drug-free and empowered for my son. This spurred me on, it gave me determination, and the faith to not give up what I felt was my ordained and human right to see my son. I am not making any excuses or blaming anyone or anything else for my plight during the 14 years that I was excluded from seeing my son. I have not got a documented criminal record; the sting of the stigma of mental health was the main reason for my abstinence from having full contact with my son for nearly a decade and a half. I hope that things have moved on regarding these stigmas, I remain an activist and as I have said, written a book about these issues previously and continue to be proud of my recovery and discovery.

Another stress drawer was actually going through a divorce which on reflection, I didn't realise how much that had taken out of me emotionally and psychologically. Again I employ people to talk to someone professionally around relationship issues. In my naïve past and my macho front, I masked my problems again as mentioned previously with drugs and other substances which did not help me regarding access and court welfare issues. Everyone handles stress and problems differently; I hope you find my own stress vulnerable model regarding the drawer analogy helpful.

I recall, prior to my last admission in August 1993 being homeless and not having any access to my son, going through a divorce, being made redundant, my brother Dave had committed suicide in January of 1993 and my grandparents passed away, I had financial problems and substance misuse issues. I was at crisis and breaking point. I hit rock bottom and was in despair; however I have reclaimed control of my life and I can do a quick recap on closing the drawer analogy. I have now got my son back in my life and on good terms with his mum, I have been clean and off substances for two decades, I have got a job that I am content in and work with a brilliant team. I have developed professionally and the radar from being a service user to a health care professional is widening all the time.

Some of the above information is backed up by Tina who wants to say something along these lines. Jason is very knowledgeable and puts a lot of enthusiasm and hard-work into service users and their families. Jason tells it how it is and instils hope back into people who are feeling lost or misguided. Jason has been very successful in helping people to get drug abstinent and towards their recovery.

Jason says, "Thanks Tina for that".

**Chapter 13: How I tackled mental illness and the crippling stigma that went with it.**

A big part of my recovery has been to overcome the sting of the stigma unfortunately associated with mental illness. I am now proud of overcoming most of these issues. In my wiser wisdom and my new life, can anybody tell me what I need to be embarrassed about? People are proud of overcoming their physical illnesses and again I reiterate what have I got to be ashamed of? I have a blog in America as follows that illustrates some of the stigmas that I endured in a less enlightened era. Thankfully I have overcome the mental health bigots to become an advocate for anti-stigma and I remain a strong activist for equality.

Imagine being called 'Frankenstein' in the street, being refused a glass of coke in a bar, your so-called friends crossing the road to avoid contact with you, humiliating laughter when you apply for a job, people whispering in a polling station that you shouldn't be allowed to vote. Not only that, but you also have a mental illness that makes you feel vulnerable and out of control; you see yourself as a social outcast.

As a former service user, I experienced all of these things and much more, having spent a part of my late adolescence and late 20's in psychiatric care as an inpatient and later as a service user in the community. I was soon to discover that the stigma I was up against was as hard to live with as the illness itself, which would destroy my self-esteem and radically reduce my quality of life for many years to come. In late December 1980, a month after turning 16 and still at school, I was admitted to Rotherham Psychiatric Unit (formally known as the Mental Health Unit, which since has been demolished, thank God!). I have described this as "A life-changing event". The direct impact of my psychiatric health problems were a significant enough blow without being compounded by the devastating aftermath of the stigma.

The stigma began to disable me in such a way that I was reluctant and embarrassed to be seen in my social environment and yet I still felt the human need for social contact. Describing myself as "A social leper", I hid myself away because of the feelings of shame and low self-esteem. My confidence was reduced to the point that I was rarely able to contact the people who had been my friends and they almost never made the effort to seek out my company; they would even cross the road in order to avoid me. There were whispers behind my back and I was even refused a glass of coke in a bar near the hospital because they knew I was an inpatient. I am glad that things have moved on. I also remember clearly the time when a group from the ward was taken to the local polling station to cast their votes. Within hearing distance, other voters discussed them in derogatory and discriminatory terms, some of them declaring that they should not have the right to vote.

I recall my first leave from hospital to a mixed reception of responses from the community. Thankfully some members of my local community saw me as "A person with problems rather than a problem person", but this attitude was not shared by everyone, including those who memorably called me 'Frankenstein' This was due to the side effects of the medication at the time, again I want to reiterate that the modern medications seem to have a better ratio of pros to cons'. Worse was to follow, when I set off to seek work on a new sewage system. As I walked into the workmen's cabin at lunch break, I was totally unprepared for the barrage of humiliating laughter that was directed at me. In stark contrast, my relatives were supportive and caring. This was in spite of their lack of experience in dealing with mental illness at the time and my feelings were that I didn't deserve their love, believing that I was a burden who had brought shame on the family and let everyone down.

Only a few months after I was discharged as an inpatient, I was re-admitted back to hospital. There, I witnessed another kind of prejudice and discrimination demonstrated by psychiatric patients against other psychiatric patients who were in some way different. Division and discrimination were commonplace on the wards, including the able not wanting to be associated with the less able, the non-violent not wanting to be associated with the violent and vice versa. The clean distancing themselves from the dishevelled, the substance users from the non-substance users, each looking down on the other, reflecting all the other divisions that exist in wider society.

I now work with people experiencing psychosis and substance issues. I think it's important that psychiatric patients have the correct advice to help minimize weight gain, or loss, resulting from side effects of medication. Not just from a physical health or self-image point of view, but to help them escape being marked, looking abnormal in a branded kind of way and becoming obvious targets for stigma.

There is help out there and I implore people to make immediate use of these services at the first sign of isolation, getting a hold of you. I should know; I am living proof that people can recover from serious mental illness and a life blighted by loneliness and stigma and that they can use their experiences to support and inform others. Again as I had mentioned before I am a big advocate of peer to peer support and the national on-going campaign Time to Change that is also been supported by celebrities who have had mental health issues. I have done my bit to support the national campaign to reduce stigma and promote awareness of mental health. I have refereed football matches, supported the campaign internally through work, I continue networking in schools, colleges, universities and various projects supporting wellbeing and other educational establishments that require a mental health input. I now feel as though my lived experience and empathy regarding the stigma and other antisocial aspects of mental illness is effective and empowering for me and those people that I hopefully make a difference to.

Here are some responses to my blog in the US and UK:

*Catrina* says:

I am a doctoral student at the University of Arkansas in the Rehabilitation education department. I would like to get in touch with Jason Tune, if possible. I am writing a journal article about mental illness and stigma, and I would like to ask him some questions about his experience. Is there a way I could get in touch with him? Thank you.

*Jason's reply*:

Hi Catrina feel free to ask me any questions about my experiences, glad to help you in your studies.

*Maggie* says:

I have found that my neighbours and others don't want to know what they know of me. I wrote my memoir and was surprised at how many of my friends did not buy it. They think I am just unpredictable. I have PTSD (Post-Traumatic Stress Disorder) and I am on Disability. I have been in treatment with my therapist for 12 years and I am really better, with a few lingering problems. The worst is anxiety, light headedness and, I guess, I am a little paranoid.

Jason's reply:

Don't worry about other people too much Maggie, after all whose life is it anyway?

*Wayne* says:

Your story is heart wrenching. I also am on disability. Where I live on a farm in the country, I don't have contact with many people but I know how judgmental they can be. I have been working very hard to get through my issues as well. My neighbours and friends now, did the same thing. I retired for the last time from a large company in 2001. Somehow one of my friends told everyone that I had PTSD from being in Vietnam. My Manager sent me to a shrink with two months disability. The following six months no one came to my office and I was not given any work to do, at all. Finally they offered me a big severance package if I would leave and not take legal action. When I see someone I know and that act strange, I just smile and say "Hope you have a nice day" even if they were trying to avoid me I would talk loud enough so everyone could hear. I have bad anxiety as well and am trying to work through it. When you're feeling down and out, she is your friend and always has time to listen. She will come through your fog of trouble, take you by the hand and lead you out. I wish you well, Wayne.

Jason's reply:

"The journey from your head to your heart is the longest and hardest journey of all" Wayne, keep at peace with yourself.

*Susie* says:

Jason is inspiring. I can see from his photo that he's now doing very well. Stigma is definitely almost as bad, if not worse than any other issue we might be facing. I think

I sensed that instinctively, and as a result I tried to keep all of my issues away from the rest of my life. In the end that didn't help me either, and just gave me other things I had to work at resolving. My family weren't supportive; they blithely overlooked my issues, even when it was pretty clear I wasn't functioning very well.

To Maggie and Wayne – this blog is a good place to share our experiences and emotions. It is possible to overcome PTSD, anxiety and other related issues. I have for the most part, save for a panic attack here and there. I wish you both much healing on your journeys!

Jason's reply:

So much empathy Susie very uncanny and so true, well said.

*Susan* says:

What an inspirational story, Jason. Yes; me too. It always seemed odd to me how I was expected to "be" normal yet was treated so differently.

In time I fully expect that as we stand and speak this will no longer be the case. In spite of this stigma it is possible to find wholeness and peace, to live a full productive life as Jason has portrayed in his story.

*A Mom's Choice* says:

As teenage Mom 16 years ago I lived with the stigma of all teenage parents are no good which was far from the truth. Too many times people are quick to judge people. I've struggled with mental illness from my own childhood nightmare for years and just now realizing just how much it's affected me. It's amazing how stereotypes can destroy people's lives. Your story was heart-warming and so true. People should see the person and not the disease. I've lived with lupus for over 8 years and I'm just now realizing that I'm not the disease it's just a part of me. Thanks so much.

Jason's reply:

I would personally like to thank all you guys out there who are speaking up and "see people as human beings with problems", rather than problem people.. God bless.

*Jane* says:

Yet again Jason gives honest and down to earth no nonsense advice learnt from his own heart wrenching and true life experiences. Jason has a wealth of information concerning mental health and the recovery of this illness. Jason is empathic in his approach and forwards a clear and concise understanding to all that request his help, this I salute Jason for. Yet again I say thank you Jason and credit to you for your relentless work and tireless help and above all for showing that there is a life for those who suffer from mental illnesses... Jane

Jason's reply:

Fantastic insight Jane and very Soulful, I believe in you too and lets all keep growing together and making a difference. 'It's a journey not a destination' and my hope is that as survivors we can help break the final taboo of stigma.

*Gary* says:

> I am a service user; this man is single handily raising the mental health stigma awareness profile from the perimeter into the main arena in his own town Rotherham, Yorkshire and beyond. Top, top, bloke, keep the ball rolling pall.

Jason's reply:

> Thank you everyone for sharing with me, it's nice to know that we are all part of the recovery movement, we are speaking up, whilst challenging some of the stereotypes, bigotry, perceptions and stigmas of mental illness. They are some very powerful messages above and I hope other people and my readers will take something positive out this.

> I am pleased to say that I am networking in schools and challenging and raising awareness of stigma and hopefully the newer generations won't be fetched up with ignorance that myself and generations before were ignorant to.

## Conclusion

People often say to me that you know best as you have been there and you understand people who are going through their own life troubles and difficulties. Yes, I agree to a point that I possibly get closer to people without the barriers in between. I often can relate to their situation and empathise and understand to a certain extent where they're coming from.

My advice to anyone in their recovery, who is thinking of using their positive experiences and empathy to help others, would be to back this experience up with some qualifications and professional education. Make sure you have a clear criminal records bureau (CRB) check as this is important when you are working with vulnerable people.

Whilst in the job role you could be working with other agencies and attending ward rounds. For example, if you are employed within an organisation you will have to work collaboratively within a multidisciplinary team. You may be expected to document patient notes and record confidential literature. Having good telephone etiquette is paramount for your professional development and credibility also. I can remember in my previous employment, as a former steel erector and demolition worker that instructions were often verbalised very loudly. Adjusting to the office environment has been a test of character and patience for me and my colleagues.

It was also noted during my interview that I had been mentally balanced for a long time and substance abstinent for over a decade. I basically had kept my nose clean and out of trouble and had turned my life round. It was important that I got supported for my job role prior to the interview off a few colleagues and family. I gathered plenty of information and research to get to know the job specifications, before I weighed the pros and cons up. I didn't go into the job with my eyes closed as I had been in my own comfort zone for a long time and I didn't want anything to rock my boat mentally.

I must admit I found it difficult initially to switch off emotionally from the clients and their situations. I got a major boost when I won an innovation award within 12 months of my new career. It has also helped me overcome from any sawdust that was left over from my psychological addiction to the mental health stigma. I have learnt a lot about the professional side of doing things, I feel as though this is part of my life's balance regarding my own mental health and I also don't want to lose my main tool of empathy, from personal experiences. My professional development has opened new doors for me, i.e., enabling me to write this book with my friend and colleague Tina. I often joke with her about coming from Wisconsin USA, fates making us meet and work together, to produce this book and have it published. We are both passionate about our roles about helping others and we continue to add our own ideas and philosophies to the recovery model of psychosis and wellbeing. I am continuing to grow and develop professionally; I feel this helps enhance my continuous journey of recovery and beyond.

"I never say I recovered because that would mean for me that there is nothing more to learn about myself and to add to my life". I would rather say as above, that I am in recovery and beyond. I want to also say that I never stop learning and developing new coping mechanisms, ideas and positive responses. I feel as though I have become more confident, the support from within work has been paramount to this confidence. I am pleased to say that the NHS Trust that I am an employee of has also given opportunities to employ other ex-service users in a voluntarily, part-time and full-time capacity. I am hoping to network more and do video diaries for schools and other educational institutions in the future. My Trust has supported some of my innovative projects, I have also appeared regularly in the Trust magazines and have had numerous articles published in the media and other magazines. I have a rapport with radio Sheffield, my local BBC radio and have been on radio across all of South Yorkshire radio stations. It's pleasing that so many people want to hear about my illness and subsequent recovery. It has proved to me that I have skills and knowledge to support and help empower other people and to empower another human being is a very empowering thing for me.

I am pleased to say that the NHS Trust is also encouraging mindfulness and relaxation groups within the employment setting. I hope that this is spread out more to service users, carers and their families, as I feel that a lot of people need to learn how to relax and switch off. I know this is easier said than done as I have experienced my fair share of racing thoughts, mania, hyperactivity induced by drug abuse and have had negative symptoms, depressive thoughts and perceptions. It has helped me think things through better; reflect more positively and given me a sense of calm.

I am very lucky that my partner Sharon helps me to meditate and relax and we often put a relaxation CD on. I have recently been on holiday to Majorca with Sharon; we found a beautiful idyllic location overlooking the sea and we would relax and meditate whilst sat on the rocks. The smells of the ocean and the sounds of waves crashing on the rocks, rays of the sun baking down on our skin was so relaxing, I have never been as chilled out before. I have now been abroad every year since my last admission to hospital in 1993 and this is something that I feel is helping me unhitch the trailer from some of my bad experiences and has helped me put my life into some perspective. I have had some really good holidays and love to get a good deal as we all do; I have got a reputation for getting a good bargain. I have to keep my big mouth shut sometimes whilst on holiday as often other holiday makers have paid a lot more than I have. I try to utilise my life experiences in many different ways, in my previous life, I was a bit of a wheeler dealer and a jack the lad, even getting a good bargain at the jumble sales with my grandma when I was a kid has been an education that I still pull on from time to time.

I don't try to justify parts of my journey as I have always taken personal responsibility for my actions and my illness as well and reflect on my past in a positive way. I believe that things sometimes happen for a reason and I feel very fortunate that I have got my humour still and often laugh in the face of adversity. I do believe that this is easier said than done now I am in recovery and beyond. It is easier for me to sit here and say that, but believe me it has been a hard, long journey and "Been no bed of roses and no pleasure cruise" as Freddy Mercury the lead singer from the band 'Queen' once sang in a song. When I take stock and just contemplate the worst thing that I could ever have done is to have wasted my life.

I feel very privileged to come out of the other side; I know a lot of people are not that fortunate. My message is never to give up hope and believe in you, try to get a positive mental attitude, looking on the bright side of life. There is help out there and if you feel the first signs of isolation, despair getting hold of you; my advice is to listen to a fool like I once was, that thought I could handle anything that had been thrown at me. I am pleased to say that I recently heard of mental health education being possibly implemented into the school curriculum in the near future. After all, we are given plimsolls, trainers, physical education kits, almost as soon as we start school; however there seems to be a lack of training for our mental side. I am involved as an extended role in my job and in my creative life networking with schools and education institutes regarding mental health, recovery and substance education. I intend to do more in the future, as I develop more partnerships as we challenge the stigma and raise more awareness.

Hopefully more people will get help at the earliest possible stage of a mental health problem. Other professionals and agencies may spot the early warning signs then refer to the appropriate services. I have had a great response recently from the NHS Trust that I am employed by, regarding my networking within education. I want to reach the broader spectrum and do more video diaries, which are short films, i.e. on You Tube, which I have already developed along with music raps, etc. I feel that people sometimes get bored of reading leaflets; people often say my videos and books are inspirational, and I feel very proud to be addressing the wider audience of society. Our service that I am working with has been involved in a promotion day at my local town football club Rotherham United FC to coincide with world mental health day in the autumn of 2013, which is the year of starting writing this book.  A professional football club supporting this project is something that I am very proud to be part of. Tina and I have been in the subcommittee that have behind the scenes to make this happen. The team has also been involved in presentations and promoting mental well-being days in schools and colleges within the Rotherham district. I am pleased to say that it shows how far we have come as a civilisation and it is great to know that we are forging more partnerships with education, thus reducing the stigma and raising awareness. Desirably establishments may identify psychosis and other mental health issues at the earliest point. I can remember when people used to hide away and some people would avoid people with mental health problems. I feel really part of the harmony within the Trust and the people that are supporting our team and extended partnerships, as this can only benefit the extensive community and beyond and empower all of us that are connected under the mental health umbrella.

**References**

The ASSOCIATE FOR COGNITIVE ANALYTIC THERAPY (2013) What's the difference between CAT and CBT? [online]. Last Accessed 2 September 2013 at http://www.acat.me.uk/page/what+is+the+difference+between+cat+and+cbt

BRITISH ASSOCATION FOR THE PERSON-CENTRED APPROACH (2013) *The Person-Centred Approach.* [online]. Last Accessed 1 September 2013 at http://www.bapca.org.uk/

BROWN Raymond and TUNE Jason (2006) *Sex, Drugs and Northern Soul.* Brentwood, Chipmunkapublishing.

CHERRY, Kendra (2013) *What is the Fight-or-Flight Response?* [online]. Last accessed 1 September 2013 at: http://psychology.about.com/od/findex/g/fight-or-flight-response.htm.

CITIZENS ADVICE BUREAU (2013) *Equality Act 2010 – discrimination and your rights.* [online]. Last Accessed 2 September 2013 at http://www.adviceguide.org.uk/england/discrimination_e/discrimination_about_discrimination_e/equality_act_2010_discrimination_and_your_rights.htm

Hert, M.D, Thys, E, Magiels, G & Wyckaert, S (2004) Anything or Nothing: Self-guide for people with bipolar disorder. Uitgeverij Houtekiet.

ICD-10 Version:2010. [online] Last Accessed 10 March 2012
at http://apps.who.int/classifications/icd10/browse/2010/en#/F31

MENTAL HEALTH FOUNDATION (2013) *Mindfulness.*
[online]. Last Accessed 11 October 2013 at
http://bemindful.co.uk/about-mindfulness/

NHS CHOICES (2012) Generalised Anxiety Disorder. [online].
Last Accessed 11 October 2013 at
http://www.nhs.uk/conditions/Anxiety/Pages/Introduction.aspx

Psychosis-bipolar.com. *Information about bipolar disorders.*
[online]. Last Accessed 10 March 2012 at http://www.psychosis-
bipolar.com/information-about-psychoses-56.html

ROYAL COLLEGE OF PYSCHIATRISTS (2001). *Beck's
original Cognitive Model.* [online]. Last Accessed 10 March 2012 at
http://bjp.rcpsych.org/content/178/41/s164.full

ROYAL COLLEGE OF PYSCHIATRISTS (2013) *Treatments &
Wellbeing: Antipsychotics.* [online]. Last Accessed 1 September
2013 at
http://www.rcpsych.ac.uk/expertadvice/treatments/antipsychoticme
dication.aspx

SCOTT, J (2001) *Cognitive therapy as an adjunct to
medication in bipolar disorder.* The British Journal of Psychiatry.
[online] Last Accessed 10 March 2012 at
http://bjp.rcpsych.org/content/178/41/s164.full

TUNE, Jason and WARBURTON, Martin (2009). *Stigma:
Worse than Psychosis.* Brentwood, Chipmunkapublishing.

ZUBIN & SPRING (1977) *The Stress Vulnerability Model. Family and Carer Information and Support Group.* [online] Last Accessed 10 March 2012 at http://sydney.edu.au/bmri/docs/stress_vulnerability_model.pdf

## Quotes from my readers

"I want to thank all my friends and readers for their reviews and comments. Wishing you all the very best" Jason.

Here are some of my reviews:

Tyrone... "What more can I say that has not already been said about Jason and both his books compulsive reading, I didn't put the books down once I had picked them up honestly the best two books I have ever read without a doubt. What an inspiration, it's an honour to know and be able to call you a friend".

Ninna... "I would just like to share some thoughts of mine, I am part way through the book Sex Drugs & Northern Soul by Jason Tune ....it is soul searching funny and a breath of fresh air just like Jason, it goes to show anyone can get well after all the trails they suffer, he's a real inspiration to others ... well done Jason xxxx".

Darren... "Hi Jason, I finished your book yesterday. It makes you realise what some people go through with these health issues. You open up your inner self to the world to help others, well done mate it's a great read".

Jane E..."I have enjoyed reading 'Sex Drugs & Northern Soul' and I think Jason is to be commended on his honesty while battling his demons head on. A personal journey through torment heartache and sheer determination has got Jason to where he is now and I applaud the good work that Jason strives to achieve in helping others in a similar dilemma as he found himself in. Well done Jason x"

Karen.... "Hi there hope your well love. Just thought I would let everyone on Facebook know how brilliant your book is 'Sex Drugs and Northern Soul' it is truly amazing and I think everyone on Facebook should read it absolutely brilliant lol".

Lorraine E....."Chez loves your book and said she would have paid 20 pounds for it, she was in tears by the second paragraph of intro, then made her smile on 2nd paragraph of your 1st chapter cause she can relate to it......well done J sounds a damn good book hehe".

Steve...Hi ya Jay. "We were at Kimmy School together, also army cadets at Aldershot etc. I've just finished your book for 2nd time, great read mate and good memories too. Glad you're now able to help others, all power to you mate. Steve (eddy) Edwards. Kimmy 1975 – 1980."

Jane L..."Everyone who grew up in Yorkshire should read this. . I was at Kimberworth Comp around the same time as J. Never judge a book by its cover - literally. Nobody realized at the time is that J was suffering from serious mental health problems which were not diagnosed until much later and were worsened by his spiral into uncontrollable drug addiction This book made me laugh a lot (as well as cry)."

Trisha..."I finished reading your book (Sex Drugs and Northern Soul) record time, 3 days, it's absolutely fantastic and I could not put it down. I recommend everyone reads this book. They'll be as engrossed in the book as I was, brought back memories of the "Good old days". This book made me laugh and cry, but proves people 'Can' change their life around for the better. Very best of luck with your next book xx."

Debs..."I have just finished reading 'Sex Drugs and Northern Soul'. I'm speechless and in shock all I can say is 'Wow' I couldn't put the book down. I was a friend of the family and I lived across the road from his nan and granddads and all I saw of J was a big friendly guy , I'm just sorry it's took so long to read it. He's made me realize that there is a light at the end of the tunnel and life is for living and you've got to make mistakes to learn from them. I saw J in hospital and I could never understand why he was there because he was such a big softy. Never knew he was such a big hit with the lady's lol . I'm so proud of you, you are one amazing man. I can't wait to get your next book". x x SWALK x x.

Martin..."I read both your books Jason very entertaining and informative, you`re an inspiration to a lot of people, had more than your fair share of problems but came through stronger than ever, a genuinely nice guy and a very good friend well done mate!"

Jayne H... My friend who has written his next book about the stigma of mental illness! "I was his nursing assistant when psychiatric departments were barbaric (back in the early 80's)! His journey at times as been very traumatic, he has now written two books. The first is 'Sex Drugs and Northern soul' (filled with every emotion, anger, love, betrayal, addiction, loss, trauma, survival, the human spirit and not forgetting his infectious humour!! and emotional intelligence etc...).Amazing true story from zero to hero! His own recovery and his insights now help a new generation with a similar disposition. A brilliant author/speaker and advocate for the recovery of mental illness. He goes from strength to strength. Keep the good work up Jason. Love that quote of yours "The human spirit is far stronger than anything that can ever happen to it" XXXX

Susan ..."Hi ya Jason started your book last night 'Stigma Worse than Psychosis' at tea time could not put it down and finished it before bed time. It was a great read gives an insight to other people's lives and your determination to get well I'm so proud of you and to others like yourself who are still trying to make it. With your help and support I'm sure many more will come through it like yourself. Got to get your 1st book now trust me to read the 2nd first lol x."

Mike...from Brighton...."Hi J, your book arrived yesterday at midday-ish...I have just completed it. I started reading yesterday evening at about six-ish. I read till about five o'clock this morning, and started again at half nine when I woke up. While reading your book from cover to cover, I have had a spag bowl, a chunk of cheese, a small peperammi, about eight cups of coffee, two cups of tea, a round of brown toast... with marmite, and about fifteen smokes. I could not put the book down until it was finished. Congratulations on getting this out. You can certainly deliver a punch. Well done on getting through these traumas of life, and for standing up for what you believe in. Once read, your story will give hope to all who are starting their own unchartered journey. I write this in full admiration of you J. All the best."

Liam…"Hello Jason I have one thing to say to you, bloody hell Tuney, Just finished reading your book, what a roller coaster and it's still on-going. I don't know if you're aware of the film that is at present in the making, about Northern Soul? On face book Northern Soul the Film. I've been an extra in it. I have to be honest I only came across your book because it had Northern Soul in in the title; I am so pleased I did what a fantastic read. Due to the film I to have been revisiting my past & I am considering writing my own book, I don't know we'll see. Stay happy. From an Old Soul Boy from Nottingham who went to Wigan Casino".

Julie…"I have just finished reading 'Stigma Worse than Psychosis' by Jason Tune, it was fantastic and it shows that people are getting more aware about this subject more. It has given me more insight of how to have coping strategies on life and inform more people of being aware of family members to understand and not just pull yourself together well done again best wishes to you and Sharon and family for a brilliant Christmas and New year x x"

Mick…"Well Jason didn't expect to think much when I read your book but how you described places and people so realistic I could almost smell the disinfectant you certainly lived loved and lost so many things you can feel your heartache but your standing tall and still living to tell your story bet your family are so proud and the people who crossed the road there loss x."

Jo…"Just been reading your book, Jesus my sides ache with laughing so many memories, I can't wait to finish it!!! East Dene Mafia what were all that about hahahah"

Cheryl D…"I did enjoy the book well done it's a great read, always fancied having a go at writing myself but fiction lol, I'm based in Doncaster I'm a ward manager in a secure hospital"

Jackie S… "Well done Jason hope your book goes well x"

Maria…"I will be buying hun. Hope you will be signing this one too xxx"

Justin Morley... Consultant Psychiatrist... "I have had the great privilege of writing a forward for a new book by Jason Tune titled 'Stigma Worse than Psychosis' which is available in both paperback and E-book from publisher Chimpunka. Jason has written courageously about his experiences of the stigma associated with a mental illness so that he can give hope to others who are in a similar position. Jason has gone from strength to strength and as he writes in the book is now working as a STAR (Support Time and Recovery) worker. Finally, for people who aren't familiar with the publisher Chipmunkapublishing, they focus (although not exclusively) on publishing books by people who have experienced mental illnesses and to quote from their site 'so that we can give more people a voice and change the way the world thinks about mental health'. I'm sure I will be hearing more about Jason's books in the future!"

Sheryl..."Good luck Jase I am so glad for you xxx hope your book goes well take care xx"

Cousin Paula... "Well done Jason!! You make the family proud xx"

Joe..."Well here it is Not as funny as last book, but made me sit up and think and realise how important it is to think before we speak, well done mate if you make a difference to one person it was worth it xxx"

Mark R... "Started ya book mate. Good read and I haven't found any spelling mistakes yet :)"

Chez Y... "I think your book 'Sex, Drugs and Northern Soul' is great. It's great to read about someone else's life in Rotherham. I read about how u pulled through depression I find it really hard to get through it I'm only 21 and been on antidepressants a year and half. I think the book is great x"

Zena..."Hi Jay, yes I read your new book and I have to say it was a great read. I felt a bit guilty really with a few things you mentioned in both your books but it was just like that at that time. How are you getting on, I think you've done great along the years well done! xx"

Donna B... "I have just finished reading 'Sex, Drugs and Northern Soul' by our very own Jason Tune.... well what can I say apart from its a privilege to know you Jay and it was great xx"

Liza B... "Fantastic first book I couldn't wait to get a spare hour so I could carry on reading...the book took you through the highs and lows of your life...very moving. Well done Jason you have come a long way... and I'm very pleased that you are living your life to the full...I've got a spare hour so I'm ...just going to start the second. I'll let you know how it goes....love always xx"

Karen Etheridge... "People just need an opportunity to be believed in and demonstrate their self-worth. Always believed in you Jason and many more people needing a break to follow their dreams. Can't wait to read the third of the trilogy of inspiration. Well done proud of you and to know you x"

Luke Tune... "Our Jason brightens every room...his big smile and presence will brighten up the darkest day and saddest mood...He has been through tough times enough for three people to endure. He's over come every tough obstacle life has thrown at him and faced every beast with the heart of a lion.....from the bowels of hell to rises of heaven, he now helps others with his own life experiences...I'm proud to call Jason my uncle and will love him till forever ends xx"

Marina Needham..." Fantastic Jason well done & good luck with your third book. Brilliant forward from Dr Hussain too :-)) Not bad going for a 'Meadowbank kid"

Philip Brailsford... "Congratulations Jason on next book, keep up the good work you are doing J, we need people like you mate who listen & help rather than ridicule & ignore, all the best pal."

Karen Wyld... "I think you are really 'Brave' sharing your experiences in the hope that you may help or inspire someone else on their Road to recovery. I agree everyone has different types of problems and each case is unique to the individual. Well done Jason I look forward to reading them all and hopefully it will help me with my own battles of life or even just open my eyes to enable me to help someone else. Good luck with your new book xx"

Linda Innes... "Can't wait for my copy, loved the other 2 and very informative, honest and inspirational xx"

David Lowe... "Well done Jase. You're an inspiration to many. The world needs people like you to drive home the awareness of an invisible illness as anyone can suffer and not realise it. Well done mate."

Iain Fox... "Good luck with the new book Jase! This message is coming to you from Wales so your books gone international!"

Kevin McCourt... "Magic pal. So pleased for you. Really looking forward to reading the next book. Enjoyed the other two and also enjoy working with you on our "little project" Let's hope that is a success also."

Karen Tune... "Well done, Jason, I'm chuffed for you! You bring a lot of hope to a lot of people. Keep up the good work love xx"

Barbara Riley... "Well done Jason, I am looking forward to your new book . ( still need to organize with a friend in UK, to send me the other two books over to NZ

Deb Hawken... Stunning... Promote your book on my page at any time. I suffered from undiagnosed acute anxiety for years and it was Spirituality that saved me. Xx"

Chris Scales... "I'll tell you what Jay, what odds would a bookie have given me in 1981 that you would've written 3 books by 49? Respect mate"

Sharon Fenton..."Proud of my lovely man xx"

Dave Scarrott..."Keep the light burning brightly pal!"

Martin Appleyard... "You go from strength to strength all respect to you pal, save me a copy J"

Patrick Tune..."Jason Tune was born in Rotherham, Yorkshire, in 1964. At 14 years of age he became a 'social outcast' finding himself part of the Rotherham drug scene. Whether this had any bearing on his mental well-being is open to debate but one would imagine, at the very least, it is partly responsible. But once he recognised his problems, it is to his own credit and his strength of character that he fought the demons that were about to destroy his life. Jason is now inspirational in his work helping other service users in Yorkshire in his day job.

Prof. Malcolm Peet, Consultant Psychiatrist..."Jason's story will be an inspiration to all those that have plumbed the depths of despair that we know as mental illness. With great personal honesty and pulling no punches, he describes his struggle to get back to a balanced life. He now works to help other people do the same."

Julie E. Sloane..."Jason's autobiography touches the heart of anyone experiencing negative periods in their life - the emotional rollercoaster and triumph from reaching out from the dark side and learning to laugh at adversity." Synonymously Jason has activated a dissent into the reduction of stigma regarding mental illness. His first book 'Sex, Drugs and Northern Soul' outlined his own recovery from his own demons and experiences as a 'service user' in the 1980's. Jason's second book 'Stigma worse than the illness', is an uplifting if not empowering story into the reduction of stigma into mental illness. No one is exempt from mental ill health vulnerabilities or immune to its susceptibilities. However Jason has become an advocate into ensuring the recovery model is perpetuated nationally, if not internationally to its maximum extent by his biography, presentation and networking."

Ray Brown..."I first met Jason through an ex-student of mine whilst bench pressing more weight than was good for my age. Out of the friendship that was formed came the idea to write the story of Jason's journey through life."

Patrick Tune..."In Rotherham, Yorkshire, on 28th November 1964 my son, Jason Tune, a healthy 10 lb baby was born. It was a normal birth without complications. I watched him grow from a happy boy into a bright teenager. As he was approaching his 16th birthday, his behaviour started to change dramatically and he became restless and withdrawn. After seeking medical advice, I was told he was suffering a mental breakdown. He spent quite a long time in an out of hospital. Despite all the trauma and stigma he encountered he never once gave up fighting to regain his identity. Through his self-belief and determination he is now able to lead a normal meaningful life. So much so, that he is now employed by a NHS Mental Health Trust helping a 'new generation' with a similar disposition."

Jason Tune & Tina Morgan